2016
Frankie
Happy Birthday
+ Happy Baking
Love the Aris

Country Calendar
Homestead Baking

Enjoy!
Allyson

Country Calendar
Homestead Baking

with Allyson Gofton

Photography by Alan Gillard
Stories by Joan Gilchrist

Contents

Our People, Their Baking

Working on this second *Country Calendar* book – in partnership with colleagues-at-arms, photographer and long-time friend Alan Gillard and pedant-scribe and writing mentor Joan Gilchrist, along with the creative team at Penguin Random House – has been a year-long project filled with exceptional experiences, which I consider myself very lucky, even humbled, to have had. I am in awe of the majestic beauty of this country and of the people who live in it and harness its resources.

This time, to celebrate the 50th anniversary of *Country Calendar* – New Zealand's longest-running television series – I directed this book towards older, more established properties, all of which have featured on *Country Calendar,* and to the long-held craft of family baking. As with the *Country Calendar Cookbook*, we found the food simple, nourishing and delicious. Busy women with families and other responsibilities on the property don't have time to fuss, and many of the recipes have, like the land, come down through the generations from a time when ingredients were limited, supermarkets non-existent and shops a day's journey or more from the farm. Our cooks are versatile, too; in the absence of the main ingredient, a sultana cake morphs into a mixed fruit cake – with or without spices!

Thus, this book opens the door and welcomes you to these families' homesteads, to find out what they bake and to learn about some extraordinary places. We met wonderful, warm, enthusiastic, inspiring and hospitable folk on our journey and learned of their deep passion for what they do and for the land on which they live; on which some families have lived for up to six or seven generations, honouring the brave pioneers who built the foundation of this country.

Five years ago the inspiration for the first *Country Calendar* book came from watching an episode of the programme that featured the Radon family, who seeded paua for a living on remote Arapawa Island, at the top of the South Island. The final shot – a director's dream – showed the family barbecuing paua on the beach, with the Interislander ferry sliding through the heads from Tory Channel as the sun set. Sitting in my suburban Auckland home, I wondered why we never enquired how they cooked the food people like the Radons produced. I did not meet them last time as they were working in Alaska – it's an amazing story on page 165 – but this year, to my joy, I did. As I stepped off the mail boat onto the Radons' pier – the only point of entry to their farm – with my son Jean-Luc, now 12, in tow, Antonia Radon was waiting to welcome me to her home. I was delighted; going to the source of inspiration is professionally and personally rewarding. Each member of my team had similar moments. For Joan, a noted equestrian journalist for whom the handsome Clydesdale horse holds a special place, visiting the stud on the windswept hills of Erewhon Station in *Lord of the Rings* country was a time to cherish (see page 208). For Alan, capturing the shepherds at work at Glenburn at sunrise reinforced why he, a London-born food photographer, chose the space and freedom of New Zealand to make his home (see page 66).

Four things stand out from the journey we took to compile this collection of stories and recipes. First, as with the previous *Country Calendar* book, there is a deep connection to the land through the generations and the sense of being today's caretakers for future generations. 'The land cannot be owned,' said one of our hosts; another, 'It's a legacy that I am part of, for me to pass on.'

Second, there is an increasing trend towards active environmental protection, more sustainable and organic methods of production, caring for the land and creating a recognisable farm-to-consumer pathway for quality produce, whether animal or vegetable.

Third, farmers and landholders are turning to tourism, not only to boost their incomes but, on some of the larger properties, to preserve the historic older buildings in which once extensive staff and their families lived. Not so long ago, most New Zealand families had a link to the countryside through family or friends but, as time – and generations – flow on, those links are disappearing, particularly with immigration of people from lands other than the traditional sources of population with no familial connections.

The development of tourism ventures on farms and stations opens up the opportunity for city-dwellers to enjoy the magic of our wonderful countryside and learn about the part of the population that provides so much of New Zealand's export income, as well as feeding them. To go from a cityscape that is always noisy and cluttered to the wide-open spaces where the loudest sounds are likely to be animals or birdsong, waves crashing or water running over rocks, where the air is clear and the night sky thick with stars is surely the best break in a frantic life.

Finally, there was an emphasis on the connection between family and dinner-time eating. In our busy lives, taking time to sit together at the dinner table and chew the fat over the day's happenings is increasingly uncommon. However, where we were welcomed, each family still maintains the traditional practice of family dinner, relishing being able to eat nourishingly without counting calories, appreciating the provenance of the food and its flavour first. I also loved their *laissez-faire* attitude to eating home baking and having a cuppa; time to taste and talk won every time!

I must thank the team at *Country Calendar* for their on-going support – executive producer Julian O'Brien, narrator Frank Torley, researcher Vivienne Jeffs, and TVNZ for allowing me the opportunity to walk into the hallowed halls of the *Country Calendar* production unit and join in. To the crew at Penguin Random House: thank you all, especially for tolerating cheerfully my many requests for picture changes, as we tried to squeeze in more photos to showcase our country and the people. Thank you to Hyundai, sponsors of *Country Calendar*, who freely loaned us vehicles to travel around the country in comfort. Heartfelt gratitude to all those families who opened their homes to us and gave us their time and their recipes.

In closing, a personal heartfelt thank you to my much-loved mentor, Tui Flower – cookery doyenne and culinary pedant – who for over 30 years has been my constant source of inspiration in the area of food writing. I went to work for Tui as a young, newly graduated aspiring chef, and learned from her how to chronicle good food and gain a deep affection and appreciation for home cooks, such as those you will meet here in this book. They truly are the source of every family's health and happiness.

Here are Our People and Their Baking. Enjoy.

Allyson Gofton, April 2016

NOTE TO RECIPES IN THIS BOOK
- **one cup of flour is equivalent to 125 grams flour**
- **eggs used are size 7**
- **cup and spoon measures are level unless otherwise stated**
- **soft brown sugar should be well-packed into cups for measuring**
- **butter used is standard and not spreadable**
- **flour used is standard plain white flour unless otherwise stated**

Map of Locations

TIME AND TIDE 26
Batley

TWO IN THE BUSH 12
Glorit

CHAOS SPRINGS 40
Waihi

OUT OF NOWHERE 104
Owhango

AN UNEXPECTED INHERITANCE 116
Te Puia Springs

HARD HILLS 52
Hunterville

CHANGING THE GUARD 130
Whangara

HERE TO STAY 78
Featherston

UPHOLDING TRADITION 146
Hastings

RUGGED COAST 90
Palliser Bay

A DREAM RUN 66
Glenburn

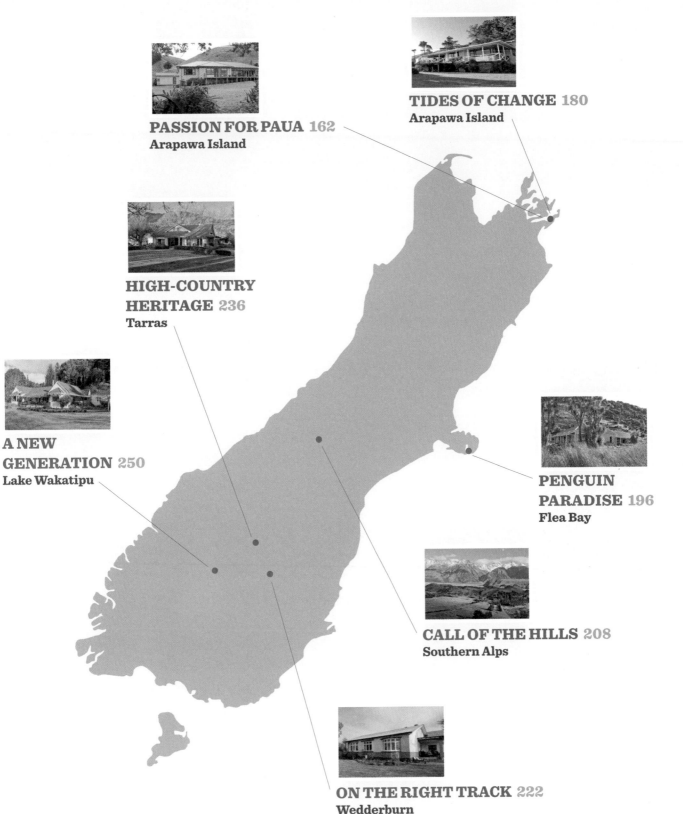

PASSION FOR PAUA 162
Arapawa Island

TIDES OF CHANGE 180
Arapawa Island

HIGH-COUNTRY HERITAGE 236
Tarras

A NEW GENERATION 250
Lake Wakatipu

PENGUIN PARADISE 196
Flea Bay

CALL OF THE HILLS 208
Southern Alps

ON THE RIGHT TRACK 222
Wedderburn

Two in the Bush

Skipping along the hallway of Mataia Homestead, little Olivia Hood has no idea that she is the seventh generation of her family on this land over the past 144 years. John Gardner II, a Scottish butcher who arrived in New Zealand in 1859, built the original homestead in 1890–91, when it became the centre of an extensive property at Glorit, southwest of Wellsford, on the edge of the Kaipara Harbour.

Nowadays the property is somewhat smaller, with some 400 acres set aside since 2006 as a conservation area and, more recently, home to a growing kiwi recovery project which Gill Adshead (née Gardner) and husband Kevin manage. Their daughter Jenny Hood (née Adshead) and husband Shane farm half of the remainder, finishing beef and lamb; the rest is leased to a dairy farmer.

Over the years, the old homestead had fallen into disrepair so for its centennial in 1991 substantial restoration was carried out on the exterior, although cost precluded continuing the work indoors or completing the landscaping. However, Jenny wanted to bring life back to the old homestead where she had grown up, the Adsheads having managed the farm for 23 years until 2003.

If Jenny's plan was to come to fruition, there was a lot of work to be done, so in 2005 it was sleeves-up for the family as they set out to recreate the ambience of an early colonial house. The old kauri floors were polished, and the bedrooms were restored – providing accommodation for up to 12 – as were the dining room with its original fireplace, a small television corner and a library room which houses a piano, old photographs and volumes of family history (including a transcript of John Gardner's diary of his voyage from Scotland). A 1969 extension on the rear of the house had added an open-plan sitting room and kitchen, plus a scullery and extra bathroom.

The grounds were later landscaped and Gill's sister, Jane Hammond, brought flowers and plants from her Auckland garden, creating a kaleidoscope of colour in the herbaceous borders. Everybody mucks in. The extensive vegetable garden and orchard produce a rich bounty – Jane comes for two days a week and she, Gill, Jenny and a friend are the gardeners and producers of jams and jellies. Kevin, with an eclectic range of skills, is the builder and maker and repairer of things.

Initially the plan was for the uninhabited homestead to become a guesthouse but Jenny says that they realised pretty quickly that people wouldn't come to Glorit on holiday, so they had to think of another way to attract visitors to Mataia and that was to create a three-day walk over the farm. However, after three years and with two young children – Emma (5) and Olivia (nearly 4) – it proved too labour-intensive for Jenny. Now the homestead is the base for a 25-kilometre two-day walk towards the nearby coast through native bush and coastal forest, with an overnight stay in a farm cottage. Next day, the walkers return to Mataia over the farm. The homestead also hosts small celebrations like special birthday parties and vintage car rallies. Kevin sees this sort of enterprise growing as more city dwellers live in apartments and want to enjoy open spaces in their downtime.

Baking at Mataia is also a family affair, with many recipes handed down the generations, and Jenny says she gained her culinary skills from Gill.

After Kevin and Gill retired, they did a two-year stint in the Solomon Islands with Volunteer Service Abroad. Gill worked as administrator at a school where her main job was encouraging and supporting the teachers, while Kevin soon found himself busy, initially building their own house and then becoming involved in projects for the poverty-stricken local community. They were remote – it was a walk of over five hours to the nearest shops – with no facilities. That experience had a profound effect on the couple. 'It changed us,' Kevin reflects, 'and when we came home, we realised that if we couldn't carry it on our backs, we didn't need it.' He built a one-bedroom cottage in the bush, where they now live, surrounded by spacious decks overlooking the Kaipara Harbour, utilising the timber from old macrocarpa trees felled near the homestead.

Now, as well as caring for the bush reserve and the kiwis, the couple spends several months a year visiting schools for the Alan Duff Duffy Books in Homes scheme. Their main focus is on the kiwi recovery project and managing the conservation area, and with Shane also passionate about conservation, the family pulls together in this venture too. So far, since the first kiwis arrived two years ago, at least five chicks have hatched successfully. A healthy, growing kiwi population will be their legacy.

'The land,' says Kevin, 'cannot be owned. It is a trust and a responsibility. We are merely caretakers who hope to pass it on in a better state than when we began.'

Bon's Pavlova

With its warm-hued crust and dense marshmallowy centre, this is a classic Kiwi pavlova that will be devoured by all who love our national pud! Gill, who for years tried many pavlova recipes with little success, said that she had given up in despair until her friend, Bonnie Armitage, gave her this recipe. Gill maintains it is the best pavlova recipe ever, with the gradual lowering of the temperature during cooking playing a major role in its success. The undecorated pavlova can be stored in a cool place in an airtight container for 3–4 days.

Prep time: *20 minutes*
Cook time: *1 hour 45 minutes*
Cooling time: *overnight*
Serves: *8*

> 3–4 egg whites, at room temperature
> 1 cup caster sugar
> 1½ tablespoons cornflour
> 1 teaspoon malt vinegar
> 1 teaspoon vanilla essence or extract

Preheat the oven to 150°C. Set the rack in the centre of the oven. Line a baking tray with baking paper.

Put the egg whites into a very clean bowl and, with the beater set to the highest speed, beat until thick and dense in texture. While continuing to beat at a high speed, very slowly add the sugar. Once all the sugar has been added, fold in – do not beat – the cornflour, vinegar and vanilla. Pile the mixture onto the prepared tray, shaping it into a round that stands about 2–3cm high.

Bake in the preheated oven for 1 hour. Do not open the oven door during cooking otherwise the pavlova may collapse. Lower the oven temperature to 125°C and bake for a further 15 minutes. Lower the oven temperature to 100°C and bake for a further 15 minutes. Lower the oven temperature to 50°C and bake for a final 15 minutes.

Turn the oven off, leaving the pavlova in the oven to cool overnight. Do not open the oven door until the pavlova is cool.

Serve topped with piles of fluffy whipped cream and, if you wish to be true to Kiwi culinary history, passionfruit pulp is a must to swirl on top.

The cold pavlova can be stored in an airtight container, away from heat and light, for 2–3 days.

COOK'S TIP
- If eggs are taken from the fridge, warm them to room temperature by placing them in a jug of warm water for 5 minutes. Cold egg whites will not beat up as well as those at room temperature.

Gluten-free Chewy Peanut Butter and Chocolate Cookies

When guests return from their night-time kiwi trek at Mataia, a warm drink and a peanut butter and chocolate cookie awaits.

Prep time: *15 minutes*
Cook time: *10–12 minutes*
Makes: *about 24 cookies*

1 cup peanut butter (smooth or crunchy)
¾ cup brown sugar
1 egg
½ teaspoon baking soda
75 grams dark chocolate, chopped into chunks (or use dark chocolate chips)

Preheat the oven to 180°C (160°C fan bake). Set the rack in the centre of the oven or, if using two baking trays, place a rack either side of the centre to ensure even cooking. Line 1–2 baking trays with baking paper.

In a large bowl, stir together the peanut butter, sugar, egg and baking soda until well mixed. Stir in the chocolate. Shape teaspoonfuls of mixture into balls and place on the prepared tray/s about 5cm apart. Press down very lightly with the back of a fork.

Bake in the preheated oven for 10–12 minutes or until lightly browned on top. Transfer to a cake rack to cool.

Stored in an airtight container, these cookies will keep for 10–14 days.

Very Easy Chocolate Sponge

Gill likes fuss-free baking and this sponge is much-loved for family birthdays.

Prep time: *10 minutes*
Cook time: *20–25 minutes*
Serves: *8*

1 cup flour, sifted
1 cup caster sugar
1 tablespoon cocoa
3 large eggs (size 7)
75 grams butter, melted
3 tablespoons milk
2 teaspoons baking powder
½ cup your favourite red jam
300ml cream, whipped
icing sugar, for dusting

Preheat the oven to 190°C (170°C fan bake). Set the rack in the centre of the oven. Grease the base and sides of two 20cm round cake tins, and line the bases with baking paper.

Place all the ingredients except the jam and cream in a large bowl and beat with an electric beater on medium speed for 3 minutes. Divide the mixture evenly between the prepared tins.

Bake in the preheated oven for 20–25 minutes or until the cakes spring back when touched in the centre. Remove from the oven, and leave the cakes to stand in their tins for 10 minutes. Turn cakes out onto cake racks to cool.

To serve, sandwich the cakes together with jam and whipped cream. Dust the top with icing sugar.

Gluten-free Chewy Peanut Butter and Chocolate Cookies

Very Easy Chocolate Sponge

Rhubarb Muffins

Many of Gill's favourite recipes come from community cookbooks, which she loves to collect. To make these muffins, Gill took a basic recipe from the *Waikato King Country Ladies Gold Association Cook Book* and made it her own by adding a spiced topping and rhubarb from her garden. The rhubarb is delicious, but when plums or feijoas are in season, Gill, Jenny or Jane will use them for a change.

Prep time: *10 minutes*
Cook time: *10–12 minutes*
Makes: *12 muffins*

2 cups flour
4 teaspoons baking powder
½ cup sugar
½ teaspoon salt
2 cups finely chopped, uncooked rhubarb
1 egg
1 cup milk
100 grams butter, melted and cooled

Topping
1 tablespoon raw sugar
1 teaspoon ground cinnamon

Preheat the oven to 200°C (180°C fan bake). Set the rack in the centre of the oven. Grease 12 standard muffin tins.

Sift the flour, baking powder, sugar and salt into a large bowl. Stir the rhubarb into the dry ingredients and make a well in the centre.

In a separate bowl, beat the egg and milk together and pour into the well. Mix gently, stirring in the butter towards the end. Mix only until combined – do not beat or over-mix as the muffins will peak like Mt Everest and be tough in texture when cooked. Divide the mixture evenly among the prepared muffin tins.

Mix the sugar and cinnamon together and sprinkle evenly over the muffins.

Bake in the preheated oven for 10–12 minutes or until well risen, golden and firm to the touch. Serve warm.

Bookie's Christmas Cake

Gardening, especially on hot summer days, is strength-zapping work. Jane, who Gill has lovingly called Bookie for much of her life, makes this cake to have on hand to revive flagging muscles. Guests at Mataia regularly ask for this recipe. Its flavoursome, moist texture makes it truly delicious and, unlike many fruit cakes, it's reasonably quick to make. Like all rich fruit cakes, it will improve on keeping.

Marinating time: *2–3 days (fruit)*
Prep time: *20 minutes*
Cook time: *2½–4 hours*
Standing time: *10 days*
Makes: *23cm cake*

450–500 grams each currants, raisins and sultanas
150-gram packet glacé peel
150-gram packet glacé cherries
¼–½ cup sherry, brandy, rum, fruit juice or ginger ale
2 cups high grade flour
1 cup soft brown sugar

150 grams butter, at room temperature
2 teaspoons ground cinnamon
2 teaspoons mixed spice
½ teaspoon nutmeg
1 teaspoon baking soda
2 eggs, well beaten
1 cup boiling-hot milk

A few days before baking, put the currants, raisins, sultanas, glacé peel and cherries in a large bowl and pour over the sherry, brandy, rum, fruit juice or ginger ale. If the dried fruit is moist, use only a quarter of a cup of liquid; if the dried fruit is very dry, use half a cup. Set aside, covered, for 2–3 days.

Preheat the oven to 140°C (120°C fan bake). Set the rack just below the centre of the oven. Grease a 23cm round or square cake tin. Place a layer of brown paper on the base of the cake tin and then place a layer of baking paper on top. Line the inner sides of the tin with baking paper. Tie several layers of newspaper around the outside of the tin; this will prevent the sides of the cake from getting overcooked.

Put the flour, sugar, butter and spices into a food processor and process until the mixture turns to fine crumbs. Transfer to a large bowl.

In a separate bowl, dissolve the baking soda in a tablespoon of milk or water and beat into the eggs. Add the egg mixture and marinated fruit to the dry ingredients and mix. Stir in the hot milk. Transfer the mixture to the prepared cake tin and use a long-bladed spatula or palette knife to level off the top. Cover with a piece of baking paper or brown paper to prevent the top from browning too much.

Bake in the preheated oven, checking the cake often after 2½ hours as it may take less or more time depending on your oven. The cake is cooked when a skewer inserted into the centre comes out clean. Remove from the oven and leave the cake in the tin to cool completely. When you remove the cold cake from the tin, keep the paper linings on the cake – this will ensure the edges do not dry out.

Store in an airtight container. This cake is best left for 10 days or so before cutting, to allow time for the cake to 'set' and the flavours to mellow.

Time and Tide

How city-born journalist Rae Roadley realised her twin dreams of love and a rural lifestyle is well documented in her book *Love at the End of the Road*, which traces her journey from town to farm and marriage to Rex.

Nowadays, Rae's home is Batley House, a stately old homestead situated on the idyllic shores of the Otamatea River, an arm of the Kaipara Harbour – and although she writes a popular column for a Northland newspaper, she's much happier in gumboots and Driza-Bone as her husband's rouseabout, than in a suit and heels!

Rex's family came to the property in 1912 when Rex's grandfather Albert and his brother Jack bought a block originally purchased from local Maori in 1839 by Thomas Spencer Forsaith, who in the 1850s led the country's parliament for just three days. The area has a turbulent history, with the father of the first European owner of the two blocks of land killed by a party of Ngapuhi warriors led by Hongi Hika; this block, along with the block Albert and Jack purchased, make up today's 1000-acre sheep and beef farm.

The Batley homestead was once a licensed hotel, post office, general store and kauri-gum trading post, serving the settlement and district, its fishermen and workers in the two mullet canning factories and the flour mill in the bay. The house overlooks the site of a former wharf used by steamers that carried passengers and goods – including fish – around the harbour. The waters off the farm are still rich fishing grounds for Rex and Rae, who enjoy catching dinner in their boat when the farm isn't demanding their attention.

Kaipara is a large district of great historical importance, all too often bypassed by travellers heading for the better-known attractions around the Bay of Islands and through the Waipoua Forest to see the remnants of a once extensive kauri forest.

The house was built as a single-storey building in 1866 by the Masefield family, but it has – in Rex's words – been a 'bitzer', having been added to in the 1870s when it was a boarding house. In 1905 it became the two-storey colonial homestead of today, although Rae and Rex have substantially remodelled the kitchen and living area.

The senior Roadleys lived in the homestead from 1919–60, and Rex was raised in one of the other houses on the farm, where his mother, Zoe, still lives. After 1960, Batley House was used by shearers, then lay empty and vandalised until it was let at a peppercorn rent as a home for disadvantaged children. Caretakers followed and, after Rex bought the house from his father and uncle, Auckland weekenders enjoyed the serenity and solitude of Batley. Since then, repairs and renovations have been carried out and now a large country kitchen is at the heart of the home.

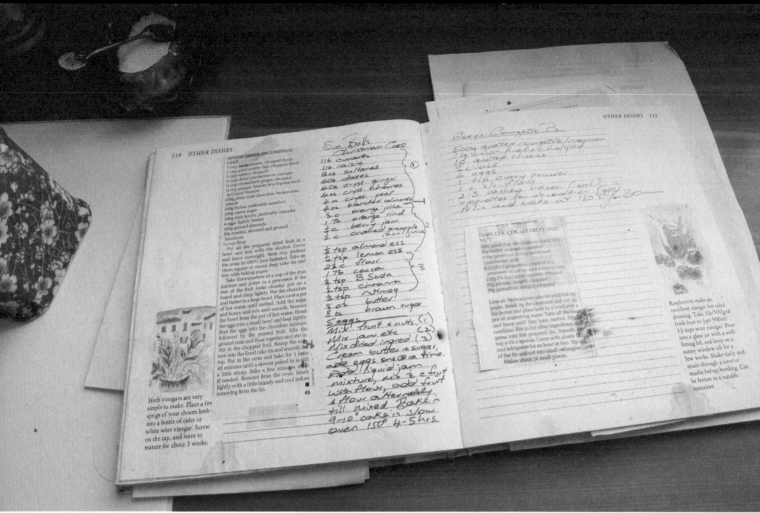

[ANZUS CHOCOLATE CHRISTMAS
CAKE]

1 cup mixed prunes, chopped finely
1 cup good-quality figs, chopped finely
1 cup raisins, chopped
¾ cup dried cranberries or currants
¼ cup crystallised ginger, chopped
¼ cup grappa, brandy or a liqueur such
  as Grand Marnier
250g plain dark chocolate, broken into
  pieces
200g butter, preferably unsalted
100g caster sugar
100g dark honey, preferably manuka
4 eggs, lightly beaten
150g ground almonds
50g roasted, skinned and ground
  hazelnuts
½ cup flour

Put all the prepared dried fruit in a
bowl and mix with the alcohol. Cover
and leave overnight. Next day, preheat
the oven to 150°C (not fanbake). Take an
18cm square or round deep cake tin and
line with baking paper.
  Take three-quarters of a cup of the fruit
mixture and puree in a processor. If the
rest of the fruit looks chunky, put on a
board and chop lightly. Put the chocolate
and butter in a large bowl. Place over a pot
of hot water until melted. Add the sugar
and honey and mix until smooth. Remove
the bowl from the pot of hot water. Break
the eggs into a small bowl and beat lightly.
Beat the eggs into the chocolate mixture,
followed by the pureed fruit. Mix the
ground nuts and flour together and stir in.
Stir in the chopped fruit. Scoop the mixture into the lined cake tin and smooth the
top. Put in the oven and bake for 1 hour
45 minutes until a skewer poked in is still
a little sticky. Bake a few minutes more
if needed. Remove from the oven, brush
lightly with a little brandy and cool before
removing from the tin.

Herb vinegars are very
simple to make. Place a few
sprigs of your chosen herb
into a bottle of cider or
white wine vinegar. Screw
on the cap, and leave to
mature for about 3 weeks.

43

Sue Bell's
Christmas Cake

1 lb currants
1 lb raisins
8 oz sultanas
4 oz dates
4 oz cryst. ginger
4 oz cryst. cherries
4 oz cryst. peel
4 oz blanched almonds
4 oz orange juice
½ c orange rind
1 Tb beet jam
½ c crushed pineapple
          + pineapple juice

½ tsp almond ess.
¼ tsp lemon ess.
2½ c flour
1 Tb cocoa
½ tsp B Soda
½ tsp cinnamon
½ tsp nutmeg
8 oz butter
8 oz brown sugar
5 eggs

Mix fruit & nuts (1)
Mix jam etc (2)
Mix dried ingred (3)
Cream butter & sugar,
add eggs one @ a time.
Add liquid jam
mixture, mix 3 e fruit
with flour, add fruit
& flour & thoroughly
till mixed. Bake in
9-10" cake in slow
oven 150° 4-5 hrs.

Joey's Courgette Pie

500g grated courgette/marrow
1 onion finely chopped
1 c grated cheese
3 c oil
4 eggs
1 tsp curry powder
1 c s/r flour
2-3 rashers bacon (opt)
tomatoes for decoration (opt)
Mix and bake at 180°C for 30 mins

DARK CHOCOLATE FRUIT AND
NUT

200g good dark chocolate, limit 70%
50g butter, preferably unsalted
250g [generous ½ cup] sweetened
  condensed milk
6 Griffin's gingernuts, crushed in a
  processor or cut up with a heavy knife
150g [½ cup] dried apricots, chopped
70g pecans, roughly chopped
70g pistachios, roughly chopped

Line an 18cm-square cake tin with baking
paper. Break up the chocolate and cut up
the butter and place both in a bowl over a
pot of simmering water. Turn off the heat
and leave until they have melted. Stir to
combine. Stir in the other ingredients and
press into the prepared tin. Smooth the
top with a spatula. Cover tin. Smooth the
and refrigerate for an hour or two. Tip out
of the tin and cut into small rectangles.
  Makes about 24 small pieces.

Raspberries make an
excellent vinegar for salad
dressing. Take 1lb/500g of
fresh fruit to 1pt/500ml!
1¼ cups wine vinegar. Pour
into a glass jar with a well-
fitting lid, and keep on a
sunny window sill for a
few weeks. Shake daily and
strain through a sieve or
muslin before bottling. Can
be frozen in a suitable
container

Rae's Easy Scones

The popularity of these time-honoured favourites lies in their simplicity and the speed of cooking. Rae refuses to make her scones into a complicated 'art form', simply adding sugar if the scones are to be served with jam, but omitting sugar if the scones will be accompanied by cheese. The addition of yoghurt gives these scones a delightful texture and taste.

Prep time: *10 minutes*

Cook time: *15 minutes*

Makes: *9 scones*

2½ cups flour
3½ teaspoons baking powder
pinch salt
about 1–2 tablespoons sugar, optional
50 grams butter, melted
1 egg, beaten
1 cup milk (or ½ cup milk and ½ cup plain unsweetened yoghurt)

Preheat the oven to 200°C (180°C fan bake). Set the rack above the centre of the oven. Line a baking tray with baking paper.

Sift the flour, baking powder, salt and sugar, if using, into a large bowl. Make a well in the centre.

In a separate bowl or jug, mix the butter, egg and milk (or milk and yoghurt) together. Pour into the dry ingredients, stirring quickly until just combined. Turn the dough out onto the prepared tray and press into a square-ish shape about 2cm thick.

Dip a large knife into water, then cut the dough into 9 squares. Push the squares apart just a little so they have room to spread while cooking. (Rae refuses to cut the dough into rounds, saying, 'It takes too much time, and it adds nothing to the flavour, so why bother?!')

Bake in the preheated oven for 15 minutes until golden. Transfer immediately to a clean, tea towel-lined basket or cake rack and serve while hot.

Date and Sultana Loaf

Fruit loaves, which stay moist and keep for ages, have never waned in popularity in country homesteads. This recipe, a favourite at Batley, is easily prepared using pantry staple ingredients.

Prep time: *15 minutes*
Cook time: *50 minutes*
Makes: *1 loaf*

4 Weet-Bix, lightly crushed
1 cup soft brown sugar
1 cup dates, pitted and roughly chopped
1 cup sultanas
50 grams butter, softened or melted
1 teaspoon baking soda
1 cup boiling water
1 egg, beaten
1 cup self-raising flour
2 teaspoons ground cinnamon
1 teaspoon ground ginger
1 teaspoon mixed spice

Preheat the oven to 180°C (160°C fan bake). Set the rack in the centre of the oven. Grease the base and sides of a medium (22cm x 9cm) loaf tin and line the base with baking paper.

Put the Weet-Bix, sugar, dates, sultanas, butter and baking soda in a good-sized bowl. Pour over the boiling water, stir, then let stand for a few minutes until cool. Stir in the beaten egg.

Sift the flour, cinnamon, ginger and mixed spice together and stir into the wet ingredients. Transfer into the prepared loaf tin.

Bake in the preheated oven for 50 minutes or until firm to the touch. Remove from the oven and allow to stand for 5 minutes before turning out onto a cake rack to cool completely.

Serve sliced and well buttered.

Rhubarb Coconut Cake

Rhubarb, a Kiwi garden perennial, grows easily at Batley and if it's not cooked and served for breakfast, it's used in this cake. With its easy melt-and-mix instructions, this cake takes next to no time to prepare.

Prep time: *20 minutes*
Cook time: *1 hour*
Makes: *20cm cake*

250 grams rhubarb
1½ cups self-raising flour, sifted
1¼ cups sugar
1¼ cups desiccated coconut
125 grams butter, melted
3 eggs, beaten
½ cup milk
½ teaspoon vanilla essence or extract
2 tablespoons Demerara sugar or coconut (use thread or desiccated)

Preheat the oven to 180°C (160°C fan bake). Set the rack in or just below the centre of the oven. Grease the base and sides of a 20cm round cake tin, and line the base with baking paper.

Divide the rhubarb in half. Dice one half finely and set aside. Cut the remaining half into 5cm lengths and set aside.

Put the flour, sugar and coconut in a large bowl and make a well in the centre.

In a separate bowl, whisk the butter, eggs, milk and vanilla together. Pour into the well and stir gently to combine.

Spread half the cake batter into the prepared cake tin. Sprinkle over the diced rhubarb and top with the remaining cake batter. Arrange the longer pieces of rhubarb on top of the cake batter. Sprinkle the Demerara sugar or coconut evenly over the top.

Bake in the preheated oven for 1 hour until golden and firm to the touch.

To serve as a dessert, accompany warm wedges of the cake with custard or whipped cream, or for afternoon tea, serve wedges of the cake lightly buttered.

Shirley Roadley's Fruit Cake

The heritage of this cake – it's from Rex's aunt Shirley, who was born prior to WWI – ensures it is a must for Christmas and special family events. It is matriarch Zoe who undertakes the job, one she says she loves.

Prep time: *1 hour*
Cook time: *2½ hours*
Standing time: *14 days*
Makes: *25cm cake*

2 cups strong black tea (cold or hot)
250 grams butter, cut into small pieces
1 cup sugar
1.5 kilograms mixed dried fruit (see Zoe's Tips)
1 teaspoon ground cinnamon
1 teaspoon mixed spice
3–4 eggs, beaten
essence of choice (such as almond or vanilla), to flavour
500 grams flour
½ teaspoon baking powder
1 teaspoon baking soda
½ cup brandy or whisky

Preheat the oven to 150°C. Set the rack in the centre of the oven. Line the base and sides of a 25cm square or round cake tin with four layers of newspaper then cover with one layer of baking paper or brown paper.

Put the tea, butter, sugar, fruit and spices in a large saucepan and bring to the boil. Lower the heat and simmer for 10 minutes. Set aside to cool completely.

Once cool, beat in the eggs and a few drops of your preferred essence.

Sift the flour, baking powder and baking soda into a separate bowl or onto a plate. Gradually add the dry ingredients to the saucepan, stirring gently to mix evenly. Transfer to the prepared cake tin.

Bake in the preheated oven for 1 hour. Lower the heat to 75°C and bake for a further 1½ hours or until the cake is well browned and a skewer inserted into the centre comes out clean. If the cake begins to brown too much, cover with a piece of baking paper or brown paper.

Remove the cake from the oven, drizzle with brandy or whisky and cover with a clean tea towel. Leave in the tin to cool completely before removing the cake. Remove the newspaper but leave the baking paper or brown paper on the cake. Wrap the cake in greased paper or baking paper and then in foil. Place in an airtight container and leave for a couple of weeks before cutting, to allow time for the cake to 'set' and the flavours to mellow.

COOK'S TIPS
- For a darker coloured cake, add 1 tablespoon molasses or 2–3 dashes of gravy browning (aka 'Parisian essence') when adding the eggs.
- Buying dried fruits separately gives a better cake than mixed dried fruit. Add finely sliced crystallised ginger and/or a few chopped glacé cherries, if wished.
- The full mixture used in this recipe makes a 25cm cake. Three-quarters of the mixture will make a 23cm cake and half the mixture will make a 20cm cake.

Chaos Springs

Not all country homesteads are stately old buildings. Take, for instance, the home of Jenny and Steve Erickson on Chaos Springs Farm, an 80-hectare property nestled between hills near the Waitawheta River, west of Waihi. New Zealander Jenny and her American husband settled back in New Zealand after living in Utah, where they operated a successful organic compost-making business and grew herbs and salad mix commercially. Theirs had been a four-year long-distance romance and when they married in 1983, Jenny agreed to live in Steve's country provided they came back to New Zealand after seven years; 'It took 20!' In the interim their daughter Sequoia, now studying in Canada, was born.

The couple initially lived in a flat above the machinery shed on the property while their impressive modern concrete home took shape over two years – mostly to their own design – utilising poplar and Lawson cypress timber and stones from the farm. The house, constructed entirely from environmental materials, is 300m^2, with in-floor heating through a big firebox and ground concrete flooring. There are two bedrooms upstairs, and downstairs are a big hallway, sitting room and a huge high-ceilinged living, dining and kitchen area. The house sits comfortably in its environment, with lots of windows for light. A huge stone chimney divides the sitting room and the main living area, and the through-and-through fireplace heats the ground floor along with a woodburner to the side of the kitchen.

'It's nice to have space. We'd always lived in small homes and wanted to spread out,' explains Jenny. 'It's a great house for a party. Sequoia's friends could come and just bunk down. When she comes home, we have Thanksgiving with a big dinner party.'

When Jenny and Steve purchased it, a third of the now organic, biodynamic property was in bush with lovely native trees, to which 7000 redwoods, 1500 lusitanicas and 700 kauri trees were added.

Jenny – a member of the Yates family, known to every keen gardener in New Zealand as supplier of seeds and gardening necessities over many generations, not to mention an indispensable book on the subject – has a degree in horticulture, and became interested in biodynamics on her OE, returning to work on an organic farm at South Kaipara, before applying the principles to their Utah property.

Now the compost-making business – started for Jenny's own purposes – has mushroomed into a successful enterprise, with most of the compost going to make liquid extracts. Steve invented a spray machine to apply the liquids because he couldn't find an efficient one . . . and now he finds himself supervising the manufacture of similar machines for clients, which are in use as far south as Wanaka!

Why Chaos Springs? 'It comes,' Jenny says, 'from the saying "out of chaos comes order". The stirring of the biodynamic preparation one way and then the other is the chaos, from which comes the order – and then there are springs on the farm.'

A lemon orchard provides fruit for sale, and there are also plum, apple, pear and blackboy peach trees. They grow garlic and seed potatoes commercially, including Maori heritage varieties. The garden is a riot of companion-planting colour with vegetables, herbs and flowers, and there's a greenhouse bulging with heritage tomatoes. The farm runs dairy grazers to use the pastures that are not under garden, potatoes and compost piles.

Jenny remembers standing by her mother when she was cooking on the family's beef farm. Jenny's own recipes reflect her love of wholesomeness, although she admits she rarely uses cookbooks any more. If she does, her favourites are Mollie Katzen's *The Moosewood Cookbook* and *The Enchanted Broccoli Forest*. The kitchen is separated from the dining room by a curved bench with a sink. Cooking is done on a big Rangemaster stove and there is a spacious open pantry. The Ericksons are pretty well self-sufficient, apart from free-range chicken and dairy, thanks to the fertile garden and Jenny's green fingers.

Tomato and Basil Loaf

Jenny has learned to be creative with the glut of tomatoes that usually greet her towards the end of summer. They taste incredible in this loaf, which is best served with fresh cheese.

Prep time: *15 minutes*
Cook time: *50–60 minutes*
Makes: *1 loaf*

1 cup Roasted Tomato and Basil Sauce (see below)
1 cup caster sugar
3 eggs, beaten
125 grams butter, softened (but not melted)

1 cup flour
1 teaspoon baking powder
1 teaspoon baking soda
½ teaspoon salt
1 cup wholemeal flour

Preheat the oven to 180°C (160°C fan bake). Set the rack in the centre of the oven. Grease the base and sides of a large (21cm x 11cm) loaf tin and line the base with baking paper.

Into a food processor, put the tomato and basil sauce, sugar, eggs and butter and process to combine. Sift the flour, baking powder, baking soda and salt together and scatter evenly over the tomato mixture with the wholemeal flour. Pulse only to combine. Transfer to the prepared tin.

Bake in the preheated oven for 50–60 minutes or until a skewer inserted into the centre comes out clean. Cool in the tin for 10 minutes before turning out onto a cake rack to cool completely.

This loaf is best enjoyed fresh, though it is also delicious toasted. Stored in an airtight container, it will keep well for about 5 days.

Roasted Tomato and Basil Sauce

Jenny uses this rich roasted tomato sauce in various ways – tossing it through pasta, adding it to casseroles or including it in her delicious Tomato and Basil Loaf (see above).

Prep time: *15 minutes*
Cook time: *1 hour*
Makes: *2 ½–3 cups*

1 kilogram ripe red tomatoes (any variety), chopped roughly
4–8 cloves garlic, crushed and peeled

2 handfuls basil leaves
2–4 tablespoons olive oil

Preheat the oven to 190°C (170°C fan bake). Set the rack in the centre of the oven.

Arrange the tomatoes in a single layer in a large dish. Scatter over the garlic and basil and drizzle over the oil. Season well with salt and pepper. Toss to mix.

Bake in the preheated oven for 1 hour. Remove from the oven and purée. Strain if wished. For a thicker sauce, Jenny suggests simmering the puréed sauce over a low heat until it reaches your preferred consistency.

Lemon Yoghurt Muffins

Fresh from the oven, these muffins have a lovely moist texture and plenty of zippy lemon flavour.

Prep time: *10 minutes*
Cook time: *10–12 minutes*
Makes: *12 muffins*

¾ cup sugar
¼ cup light-flavoured oil (Jenny uses canola)
1 large egg (size 7), beaten
1 cup low-fat plain unsweetened yoghurt
grated rind of 1 large or 2 small lemons
¼ cup lemon juice
pinch salt
2 cups self-raising flour, sifted

Glaze
2 tablespoons icing sugar
1–2 teaspoons lemon juice

Preheat the oven to 200°C (180°C fan bake). Set the rack in the centre of the oven. Grease 12 standard muffin tins or line with paper cases.

In a large mixing bowl, stir together the sugar, oil, egg, yoghurt, lemon rind and juice, and salt. Carefully, without over-mixing, add the flour and stir gently to make a soft, thick batter. Divide the mixture evenly among the prepared muffin tins.

Bake in the preheated oven for 10–12 minutes or until well risen and firm to the touch.

While the muffins are cooking, prepare the glaze by stirring the icing sugar and lemon juice together (there's no need to heat).

Once the muffins are cooked, remove from the oven and let stand for 4–5 minutes before brushing with the glaze.

Serve warm.

Jenny's Apple Crisp

With apple trees flourishing at Chaos Springs, this trusty family favourite is often on the menu. Jenny likes to use her La Chamba cookware – it's both direct heat-proof and ovenproof, making cooking very easy. Apple crisp is the American name for apple crumble; Jenny's version is packed full of delicious nuts and seeds.

Prep time: *30 minutes*
Cook time: *35–40 minutes*
Serves: *6–8*

Apple Filling
12 small red-skinned apples (or use 5–6 large apples)
½ cup apple juice
½ cup raisins, sultanas or currants
6–7 whole cloves
1 tablespoon ground cinnamon
1 teaspoon grated nutmeg
brown sugar or honey to taste, optional

Crisp
¼ cup ground almonds
¼ cup breadcrumbs (white or wholemeal)
¼ cup wholemeal flour
2 tablespoons sesame seeds
2 tablespoons sunflower seeds, untoasted
1 tablespoon soft brown sugar
3 tablespoons light-flavoured oil or melted butter

Preheat the oven to 180°C (160°C fan bake). Set the rack in the centre of the oven.

To make the apple filling, peel and core the apples. Jenny only ever peels half of the apple as she likes the colour and flavour the skins impart. Cut the apples into chunky slices.

Place the apple slices, apple juice and raisins, sultanas or currants with the cloves, cinnamon and nutmeg in a saucepan. Cook over a moderate heat for about 10 minutes, turning regularly until the apples are half-cooked. Sweeten with brown sugar or honey, if wished. Transfer the apples to a 6–7-cup capacity ovenproof dish.

To make the crisp, toss together the ground almonds, breadcrumbs, wholemeal flour, sesame and sunflower seeds, sugar and oil or butter. Scatter over the top of the hot apples.

Bake in the preheated oven for 35–40 minutes or until the crisp is just nicely browned and the apple juice is beginning to bubble up around the edges.

Allow to stand for 10 minutes before serving, as the apples will be burning hot. Serve with ice cream or cream, if wished.

Hard Hills

Sheep and cattle are the lifeblood of the Duncan family's four farms, but at the home farm, Puketoi in the Turakina Valley 20 kilometres west-northwest of Hunterville, horses and food dominate. The family are Ken and wife Jacques and teenagers Harry, Jimmy-James and Georgina. Puketoi was originally part of a much larger property, Otairi (now farmed by Ken's brother Doug), which was bought by pioneer Duncans from local Maori in 1881.

Ken – who took over his grandfather's Romney sheep stud – is hopeful that his children will carry on a tradition that has seen generations on this land and the Duncan name prominent not only in farming, but in civic, community and thoroughbred racing circles over the years.

Jacques came to work for Ken, who was an international polo player, and never left. They've been married for 20 years. The whole family rides – both Harry and Georgina have had success in pony show jumping, and their winter sport is riding to hounds with the Rangitikei Hunt, which Ken says gives the youngsters the balance and skills to ride steep country when working stock.

The Duncan homestead was built with timber from the estate and, says Jacques, 'everything was rimu . . . too much brown . . . men seem to like brown!' She oversaw the conversion of three rooms into a big, bright dining and living room, overlooked by the kitchen, which opens out onto a deck. The dining table, dresser and cutlery canteen came from the original homestead at Otairi and many historic family photographs adorn the walls down the hallway. The garden, she says, has been much simplified from earlier times when the Duncan ladies were 'great gardeners', and the vegetable patch has been abandoned in favour of riding horses.

When Jacques set off for her OE from Tamworth, New South Wales, she planned to work with horses but finished up as a nanny in a large house in Scotland. Her employer owned a catering company. 'I had no idea about cooking,' she recalls, 'but she was very patient and taught me.' Not surprisingly, Jacques' favourite cookbooks are by Scottish food writer Lady Claire Macdonald of Skye, a friend of her employer.

'Turakina is a very social valley, so everyone is a good cook,' says Jacques. 'Nobody around here goes to restaurants because it's too far to go; that means lots of entertaining and socialising.' Events like the local horse sports and dog trials held in the front paddock bring lots of mouths to feed. Duck features a lot on the Duncan menu – 'Shooting is a religion around here,' she laughs. She relies a lot on her freezer, doing her shopping wherever she happens to be. The men also shoot deer and pigs.

Jacques also cooks for the big horse coach that carries the horses and family to shows, race days and hunting. On race days everyone, including Ken's mother Jean, aged 80, piles into the truck. Wherever the truck parks, Jacques loves having visitors, for whom she provides tasty nibbles. There are always cakes, biscuits and slices in jars on a shelf for the kids to snack on – no junk food here. To stock the truck for overnight trips, Jacques prepares roasts and pies with vegetables to reheat; the truck also boasts a pull-out barbecue and drinks fridge. No wonder it's a magnet for family and friends.

Ken has his owner–trainer's thoroughbred racing licence and, in a fairytale story, won the prestigious 2014 Great Northern Hurdles race with the first racehorse he and Jacques owned. Wee Biskit, by a son of the legendary Zabeel, was bought for $200 on TradeMe as a potential polo pony, but her knee action was too high. She didn't fire from a professional stable, so Ken brought her home to train and she immediately showed ability. He thought it might be a bit cheeky entering her for the big Auckland hurdles, but the little mare finished the race, on appallingly wet and heavy ground, running away from the rest of the field by eight lengths. Perhaps one of the secrets to Ken's training success is that he sings to his horses as he works with and rides them!

One-bowl Banana Cake

Banana cake is a perennial favourite with most Kiwi families, and Jacques' version is quick and easy to prepare and ideal for kids to make. Jacques often doubles the recipe to make two cakes, joining them with either Lemon Butter or Basic Cream Cheese icing (see recipe on page 265).

Prep time: *15 minutes*

Cook time: *40–45 minutes*

Makes: *20cm cake*

2 ripe bananas, well mashed
1½ cups sugar
2 eggs
125 grams butter, very soft but not melted
½ cup plain unsweetened yoghurt
2 cups self-raising flour, sifted
½ cup chopped walnuts, optional

Preheat the oven to 180°C (160°C fan bake). Set the rack in the centre of the oven. Grease the base and sides of a 20cm round cake tin and line the base with baking paper.

In a large bowl, beat together the mashed banana, sugar, eggs, butter and yoghurt. Stir in the sifted flour and add the walnuts, if using. Transfer to the prepared cake tin.

Bake in the preheated oven for 40–45 minutes or until a skewer inserted into the centre comes out clean. Leave in the tin for 10 minutes before turning out onto a cake rack to cool.

When cold, ice as wished or serve simply dusted with icing sugar. If not iced, this cake will keep for 5–6 days in an airtight container. Once iced, it is best consumed within 4–5 days.

Chocolate and Cinnamon Cream Pie

From her time living and working in Edinburgh, two cookbooks by well-known Scottish food writer Claire Macdonald became Jacques' recipe bibles. This dessert pie recipe adapted from one of the books, *More Seasonal Cooking*, includes generous amounts of cinnamon to enhance the flavour of the chocolate. Once made, the pie freezes well, making it ideal to have on hand for unexpected guests.

Prep time: *40 minutes*
Cook time: *20–25 minutes*
Chill time: *3–4 hours*
Serves: *8*

Pastry
1¼ cups flour
100 grams butter, chilled and diced
¼ cup icing sugar
few drops vanilla essence

Filling
1¼ cups milk
175 grams dark chocolate, chopped
⅓ cup caster sugar
2½ teaspoons ground cinnamon
1½ teaspoons cornflour
3 large egg yolks
1 tablespoon gelatin
¼ cup cold water
300ml bottle cream, chilled

Preheat the oven to 180°C (160°C fan bake). Set the rack in the centre of the oven. Grease the base and sides of a shallow-sided 23cm loose-bottom flan tin or similar.

To make the pastry, put the flour, butter, icing sugar and vanilla essence into a food processor and process until the mixture forms moist crumbs. Press into the base and up the sides of the prepared tin. Line with baking paper and fill with baking blind material.

Bake in the preheated oven for 20–25 minutes or until the pastry is well cooked. The pastry will be cooked when the edges are lightly browned and the pastry is firm and looks dry. Remove the baking paper and baking blind material and allow the pie shell to cool.

To make the filling, put the milk and chocolate in a saucepan over a low heat, stirring until the chocolate has melted.

Mix the sugar, cinnamon, cornflour and egg yolks together and pour into the hot milk, stirring quickly and continuously until the custard thickens. Remove from the heat.

Stir the gelatin and water together and pour into the hot custard, stirring well until the gelatin dissolves. Place a layer of plastic wrap on top of the custard; cool.

When the custard is very cool, but before it begins to set, gently whip the cream to soft peaks and stir carefully into the custard. Pour into the baked pie shell, spreading out to create a smooth top. Refrigerate for 3–4 hours until set.

If wished, top with extra whipped cream and decorate with broken pieces of chocolate to serve.

Orange Biscuits

Another favourite of Jacques'. Like many of her recipes, this one also hails from Scotland.

Prep time: *20 minutes*
Cook time: *12–15 minutes*
Makes: *about 24 biscuits*

2 cups self-raising flour
¾ cup caster sugar
175 grams chilled butter, grated
grated rind of 2 oranges
2 large egg yolks

Topping
2 egg whites
extra caster sugar for sprinkling
150–250 grams dark chocolate, optional

Preheat the oven to 180°C (160°C fan bake). Set the rack in the centre of the oven or, if using two baking trays, place a rack either side of the centre to ensure even cooking. Grease 1–2 baking trays or line with baking paper.

Sift the flour and sugar into a large bowl and rub in the butter until the mixture resembles fine crumbs. Use a dinner knife to cut the orange rind and egg yolks into the crumb mixture. Once the mixture forms large clumps, turn out onto a lightly floured bench and bring the mixture together, kneading lightly. Roll the dough out to 0.5cm thick. Cut into your preferred shapes and place on the prepared tray/s, leaving room for the bisuits to spread.

To make the topping, use a fork to whisk the egg whites until they begin to froth. Brush the biscuits with the egg white and sprinkle with caster sugar.

Bake in the preheated oven for 12–15 minutes or until the biscuits just begin to colour on the edges. Transfer to a cake rack to cool.

For jaffa biscuits, chop the chocolate and melt in the microwave or in a bowl over a saucepan of simmering water. Spread or pipe decoratively on top of each biscuit.

Store the biscuits in an airtight container. These buttery biscuits will keep well for 10–14 days.

Dream Bars

Jacques always has a stash of these rather indulgent and delicious bars in the biscuit tins that fill the shelves in the family's horse truck, ready for hungry teenagers and their friends to devour.

Prep time: *15 minutes*
Cook time: *25–30 minutes*
Makes: *20 pieces*

175 grams plain sweet biscuits, finely crushed
75 grams butter, melted
150 grams dark chocolate, chopped (or use chocolate chips)
1–1¼ cups dates, pitted and chopped
½ cup dried apricots, finely chopped
⅔ cup desiccated coconut
½ cup flaked or sliced almonds
395-gram can sweetened condensed milk

Preheat the oven to 180°C (160°C fan bake). Set the rack in the centre of the oven. Grease a 27cm x 18cm cake tin, or one of similar size, and line the base and sides with baking paper.

Mix together the biscuit crumbs and butter and press into the base of the prepared tin. Scatter over the chocolate, dates, apricots, coconut and almonds. Drizzle over all of the condensed milk.

Bake in the preheated oven for 25–30 minutes or until the top of the slice is golden brown. Leave in the tin to cool.

Once cool, cut into pieces and store in an airtight container. These bars will keep well for about 7 days. To keep longer, store in the refrigerator.

A Dream Run

John and Helen McFadzean had both dreamed of owning a large station since before they met, when they were still in their teens; John as a youngster reading about sheep stations, Helen focused on the high country and horses. Fast-forward several years . . . John and Helen, married with three sons and a daughter, are highly respected farmers of Glenbrae at Carrington, near Carterton, although the dream of big station life still lingered. In 1998, they found their ideal property when Glenburn Station at Te Wharau, east of Masterton, came up for auction, but they were outbid by an American investment company. However, to their surprise and delight, the Americans bailed out after several years, and in 2007 the McFadzeans were able to buy the station.

Glenburn has been farmed since 1873. It was bought by Edward 'King' Riddiford in 1900 to add to already substantial landholdings, and was inherited by his successors. In 1907 Riddiford built the homestead of kauri, native rimu and matai, shipped around the coast and floated ashore. It's a handsome six-bedroom villa, with high studs and a verandah set amid karaka, walnut and copper beech trees, with a view of the Pacific Ocean. The woolshed, stables, workshop, implement and hay shed, three staff houses and two baches lie slightly to the south and east of the homestead, and are all painted 'Glenburn green' and cream. The manager's home for many years, the homestead has been modernised inside, but its essential design and character have been retained.

In the early days Glenburn supported a big staff, but mechanisation and economics have seen the numbers much reduced, leaving empty houses. The McFadzeans have modernised four of these dwellings, turning them into visitor accommodation and they, along with the homestead, cater for up to 60 guests. It's an idyllic spot for family or groups to holiday, with spectacular views, rich fishing, coastal and farm walks, diving and snorkelling, and the experience of life on a working farm.

Helen runs the accommodation, while John, their younger son Lachie and two shepherds do the farming and stock work. Eldest son Johnnie and his family now run Glenbrae. Daughter Tessa is in Auckland in a marketing role with Fonterra; third son, Corey, a university graduate, is completing teacher training.

The 3000-hectare Glenburn Station carries 13,000 head of stock (17,000 stock units). It has a sheep flock of 6900 Romney ewes and 2300 replacement hoggets, with all lambs being finished on the farm. The two family farms, Glenburn and Glenbrae, produce 14,000 lambs annually for sale. John likes his cattle and together the two properties run 1000 breeding cows. For over 30 years his 460-strong Glenbrae Angus herd has topped the weaner steer sale at Masterton and albeit less frequently has achieved the highest price in New Zealand. The two-year-old steers and heifers from Glenburn are sold as quality Angus Pure beef. Farm policy means a rigorous bull selection process to ensure good genetics and conformation in the stock.

Then, of course, there's what John refers to as the 'Back Paddock', the sea on their doorstep. 'We've got approximately 1.2 million crayfish, 3 million paua, 800,000 butterfish, 1.2 million blue cod, as well as tarakihi, groper, moki and trumpeter.' It's a rich coastline, protected by private ownership, and is a breeding ground for many species. Not surprisingly, seafood is a major feature on the family menu – it's no problem to pop out in the boat and catch dinner in the evening!

Helen has two vegetable gardens, and keeps hens and a couple of pigs. Members of HelpX (a volunteer work exchange website) help out in the height of the season with cleaning and odd jobs. One might be forgiven for thinking that living in such a remote corner, an hour's drive from Masterton, could get lonely – but between holidaymakers, walkers, riders, hosting weddings and visits from service groups such as Probus, Rotary and the like, there's never a dull moment for the McFadzeans. Helen tries to get into town weekly for supplies, but what she doesn't get, the postal service brings in.

John and Helen's dream became their reality, and they never cease to appreciate living on an iconic property with views to die for and the opportunity to create a legacy for the next generations.

Peanut Chews

These are a favourite with the shearers and backpackers who come to work at Glenburn. Helen likes recipes such as this one that use pantry staples and keep well.

Prep time: *15 minutes*
Cook time: *15–20 minutes*
Makes: *about 24 pieces*

125 grams butter
¾ cup sugar
1 tablespoon milk
1 tablespoon golden syrup
1 cup flour
1 teaspoon baking powder
1 cup Rice Bubbles
1 cup blanched peanuts (raw or roasted), roughly chopped

Preheat the oven to 180°C (160°C fan bake). Set the rack in the centre of the oven. Grease a 20cm x 30cm slice tin and line the base and sides with baking paper.

Heat the butter, sugar, milk and golden syrup in a saucepan over a low heat until the sugar has dissolved. Alternatively, use a microwave: place all the ingredients into a microwave-proof bowl and heat on high for about 1 minute or until the butter has melted. Stir to mix well.

Sift the flour and baking powder into a bowl and stir through the Rice Bubbles and peanuts. Add the wet ingredients and mix well. Press into the prepared slice tin.

Bake in the preheated oven for 15–20 minutes or until golden in colour.

Mark into bars while warm. Cut when cold.

Stored in an airtight container, these peanut chews will keep for 2–3 weeks.

VARIATION
- Add a chocolatey note by using Coco Pops instead of Rice Bubbles.
- For a glamour touch, use macadamias or pistachios instead of peanuts.

COUNTRY CALENDAR HOMESTEAD BAKING

Glenburn Sultana Cake

Helen recommends making this cake a couple of days in advance of eating, to allow the cake time to 'firm up' before cutting. Often she will add a little mixed spice or grated nutmeg for flavour, or if the sultanas are sparse, she will make up a mix of whatever dried fruits are to hand. Flavourings like citrus rinds and essences can also be added.

Prep time: *30 minutes*
Cook time: *1½ hours*
Makes: *20cm cake*

500 grams sultanas
250 grams butter, diced
1 cup sugar
juice of ½ lemon
3 eggs, beaten
2½ cups flour
1 teaspoon baking powder

Preheat the oven to 180°C (160°C fan bake). Set the rack in or just below the centre of the oven. Grease the base and sides of a 20cm square cake tin and line the base with baking paper.

Place the sultanas in a saucepan, adding sufficient water to just cover the sultanas. Bring to the boil, lower the heat and simmer for 5 minutes, then strain.

Stir the butter into the hot sultanas and, once the butter has melted, allow the mixture to cool a little. Beat in the sugar, lemon juice and eggs. Sift the flour and baking power together and stir through the sultana mix. Transfer to the prepared cake tin.

Bake in the preheated oven for 1½ hours or until a skewer inserted into the centre comes out clean. Cool in the tin for 15–20 minutes before turning out onto a cake rack.

When cold, store in an airtight container. This cake will keep for about 2–3 weeks.

Serve iced with a simple lemon icing (such as the one on page 265), if wished.

COOK'S TIP
• In place of icing, scatter a handful of sesame seeds, oat bran or desiccated coconut over the cake batter before baking.

Raspberry and Rhubarb Custard Crumble

Rhubarb goes well with berry fruits – strawberries, raspberries, blackberries – which Helen keeps plenty of in the freezer for easy entertaining all year round. All of these fruits partner with custard, so rather than thickening the fruit juices with cornflour, Helen simply tosses the fruit with custard powder. This thickens the fruit juices and adds a hint of vanilla-custard flavour.

Prep time: *20 minutes*
Cook time: *40–50 minutes*
Serves: *6*

8–10 stalks rhubarb, trimmed and chopped
3 cups raspberries (if frozen, no need to defrost)
½ cup sugar
1–2 tablespoons custard powder

Crumble
1 cup rolled oats
1 cup soft brown sugar
¾ cup flour
150 grams butter, softened and diced

Preheat the oven to 170°C (150°C fan bake). Set the rack in the centre of the oven. Lightly grease a deep lasagne-style dish or 6 individual ramekins.

In a large bowl, toss the rhubarb and raspberries with the sugar and custard powder. Frozen fruit releases more juice while defrosting, so you may need 2 tablespoons of custard powder if using frozen raspberries. Transfer the fruit to the prepared dish or ramekins.

To make the crumble, mix together the oats, brown sugar and flour. Rub in the butter until the mixture looks like crumbs. Scatter over the fruit.

Bake in the preheated oven for 40–50 minutes or until the crumble is golden and the fruit bubbling.

Dust with icing sugar and serve with custard, yoghurt, cream or ice cream.

Here to Stay

EST 1850

WAIORONGOMAI
STATION

Charlie Matthews is the sixth generation of his family to farm Waiorongomai Station in the Wairarapa, between the Rimutaka Ranges and Lake Wairarapa. He and his wife Karla have two sons, Josh (14) and Willie (12), and a daughter, Greta (10), and they hope that the youngsters will love the place as much as they do, and that another generation of Matthews will follow them – although there will be no pressure. 'It is about the here and now, not the future. You don't appreciate living on a place like this until you are older,' says Karla. The couple married in 2000 in the little memorial church built by the Matthews family for the district, where services are held on special occasions, as well as baptisms and weddings.

Waiorongomai is 3000 hectares, of which 1550 are farmed; the remainder is in bush and swamp. Stock units number some 15,000, including 6000 Romney ewes and the country's oldest registered pedigree Romney stud, established in 1875 by the second Matthews generation, Alfred. The original pioneers, Charles and Elizabeth, started farming Waiorongomai in 1850, droving sheep around the coast from Wellington. There is also a commercial beef herd comprising various breeds.

The original 29-bedroom homestead, built of timber milled in the hills, was demolished in 1927. 'I would have loved to have walked through it just once,' says Karla, 'but I wouldn't have wanted to live in it!' The old house survives through its timber, which was used to build a new homestead on the same site. The house may be more modern, but history is evident in the surrounding old trees, which are home to a rich birdlife. The past resonates through paintings, photographs, memorabilia, papers and books. History is kept alive and past generations are still a part of the life.

Charles and Elizabeth had seven children, the first of whom died aged 9 months on the ship from England in 1842, and only two survived into adulthood. Charlie's parents, Raymond and Susie, have now retired to town, while the present generation has a modernised four-bedroom house, with a big open family area where the dining table sits between the kitchen and the seating area with its big picture window.

In the past, with over 100 people living on the station, a big vegetable garden and orchard fed everyone. It's more modest now, in the absence of the full-time gardener once employed. The extensive gardens around the two homesteads have hosted garden walks and weddings.

Rather than let former staff houses disintegrate, Karla oversaw the refurbishing of the older homestead and two other cottages. The accommodation is varied: the homestead sleeps 21, while the others are more modestly sized. Adjacent to the homestead is a little old corrugated-iron one-bedroom cottage. Karla, who hails from Otago and was a neonatal nurse, also takes care of the stud records and farm administration. Charlie is more of an outdoorsman and escapes to the bush when he can. He loves the land and the bush, being out with his dog, hunting or just enjoying the tranquillity, the birdlife and his surroundings.

Reflecting on what Charles and Elizabeth achieved when they first cleared the land with only the most basic tools, Charlie feels a strong element of his life on this land is as caretaker, one of a long line with the same values. 'I feel privileged to be here now, but there's also a responsibility to preserve Waiorongomai in a way that honours all the hard work of earlier generations. It's a legacy that I am part of, for me to pass on.'

WHARE GULLY
ZAMBI
CAMERONS
SPLASH
SAWPIT
REEF GULLY
TED JAKE
TAYLORS
WAIO HUTT
BOOT BUTTER
GREENS
TOP DI

Farmhouse Biscuits

At Waiorongomai these biccies, which are similar to Anzac biscuits, are often included in the kids' lunchboxes.

Prep time: *15 minutes*

Cook time: *20 minutes*

Makes: *about 24 biscuits*

1 cup rolled oats
1 cup desiccated coconut
½ cup sugar
½ cup flour
½ cup white chocolate chips or drops
1 ½ teaspoons baking soda
2 tablespoons hot water
2 tablespoons butter, melted
1 tablespoon golden syrup

Preheat the oven to 160°C. Set the rack in the centre of the oven or, if using two baking trays, place a rack either side of the centre to ensure even cooking. Grease 1–2 baking trays with butter or line with baking paper.

In a bowl, stir together the rolled oats, coconut, sugar, flour and chocolate.

Dissolve the baking soda in the hot water. Stir the butter and golden syrup together. Add the wet ingredients to the dry ingredients and stir to mix well.

Mould spoonfuls of mixture together and place on the prepared tray/s. Flatten gently with a fork, leaving room for the biscuits to spread.

Bake in the preheated oven for 20 minutes or until lightly golden in colour. Transfer the biscuits to a cake rack to cool.

When cold, store the biscuits in an airtight container. They will keep well for two to three weeks.

'Tuck Box' Honey Shortbread

Bees enjoy the wild flora that cover the outer reaches of Waiorongomai, producing an intensely rich-tasting bush honey. Karla likes to use the honey when she makes shortbread: it adds a unique twist on the classic recipe.

Prep time: *15 minutes*
Chill time: *30 minutes*
Cook time: *25 minutes*
Makes: *24–30 biscuits*

250 grams butter, at room temperature
½ cup icing sugar
¼ cup mellow-flavoured honey (try orange blossom, manuka, rata or pohutukawa)
1 cup cornflour
2 cups flour

Preheat the oven to 150°C. Set the rack in the centre of the oven or, if using two baking trays, place a rack either side of the centre to ensure even cooking. Grease 1–2 baking trays or line with baking paper.

Beat the butter and icing sugar together until light in colour and creamy in texture. Beat in the honey. Sift the cornfour and flour together and work into the creamed mixture to make a soft, but not sticky, dough. Turn out, bring together and wrap in plastic wrap. Refrigerate for at least 30 minutes, to allow the dough to firm up a little.

On a lightly floured bench, roll the dough out to 0.5cm thickness and cut into your preferred shapes. Place on the prepared tray/s.

Bake in the preheated oven for about 25 minutes or until lightly golden. Transfer to a cake rack to cool.

Once cool, store the shortbread in an airtight container, where it will keep for 10–14 days. These biscuits will taste even better if left for 3–4 days before eating.

Lemon Brownie

Butter, lemons and eggs – used here in decadent proportions – bake their way into a stunningly moreish brownie that will be hard to resist. It's an often-requested dessert in Karla's family when the lemon tree is heavy with its annual crop.

Prep time: *20 minutes*

Cook time: *25 minutes*

Serves: *8*

1½ cups flour
1½ cups sugar
250 grams butter, softened
4 eggs, at room temperature
2 tablespoons grated lemon rind
¼ cup lemon juice

Preheat the oven to 180°C (160°C fan bake). Set the rack in the centre of the oven. Line the base and sides of a 20cm x 30cm slice tin with baking paper. (If wished, use a smaller tin to make a thicker brownie.)

Using an electric beater, beat the flour, sugar and butter together until well combined.

In a separate bowl, whisk together the eggs, lemon rind and juice. Pour the egg mixture into the creamed mixture and beat at a medium speed for 2 minutes until smooth and creamy. Do not fret if at first the mixture looks curdled – continue beating and it will come together. Pour into the prepared tin.

Bake in the preheated oven for 25 minutes or until golden in colour and just firm to the touch (if making a thicker brownie, allow an extra 5 minutes' cooking time). Allow to cool for 15–20 minutes before removing from the tin.

Serve dusted with icing sugar and, as this is very rich, cut into small pieces. If serving for a dessert, accompany with a Greek-style yoghurt to cut through the sweetness of the brownie.

Rugged Coast

There's no grand homestead at Kawakawa Station on the southernmost shore of the North Island, overlooking Palliser Bay. Instead, a modest corrugated iron farmhouse filled with laughter and love, family memorabilia and the inevitable chaos that goes with two young children is the heart of the property farmed by Duncan and Sarah Furniss.

The Furniss family – Duncan, his father and late mother – came here 14 years ago after farming in the Waikato and Manawatu. Duncan had spent a number of years on South Island high-country stations and loved that wild land. He says that Kawakawa was the furthest south he could persuade his parents to move! He had met an English lass who was working in the pub at Glenorchy at the head of Lake Wakatipu. Seven years later Sarah, who trained as a chef and ran nightclubs in England, came to Kawakawa – and never left. Now, with Duncan's father living in Masterton, the couple juggles the demands of earning a living with caring for Isla (4) and Finn (2).

The farm isn't only about sheep and cattle; it is host to the Kawakawa Station Walk, which sees outdoor enthusiasts embark on a three-day trek. The overnight huts, to which luggage and food are delivered each day, are comfortable, modern and cheerful, solar-powered and heated by wood-burning stoves. More primitive is the 'Black Hut' used by hunters, the walls of which are papered with old newspapers dating as far back as the nineteenth century.

Before children, Sarah did everything, but now she attends to the books, the bookings and promotion. The walkers' food is prepared by a local chef; it has to withstand being bumped around the steep hills and through the stony riverbed of the Otakaha Stream that runs down the valley.

Duncan much prefers being outdoors to dealing with paperwork, whether he's working, hunting deer or just taking time in the extensive bush on the property. 'He'd rather fence the whole farm by hand than do DIY at home!' says Sarah. 'WWOOFers (Willing Workers on Organic Farms) are great for doing jobs we haven't got time to do ourselves.' A nanny helps out during the walking season, while Sarah services the huts. 'People think because we live remotely, we never see anyone . . . but it's quite the opposite. We have to go away to get a bit of peace!'

The farm, dating from 1847, is almost 3000 hectares, carrying 3000 sheep and 300-plus Angus cattle. The Furnisses' philosophy is to take care of the soil and the feed will look after itself, so instead of applying nitrogen fertiliser, they use dicalcic phosphate. They say the result is healthier animals and pasture that doesn't dry off as quickly in drought and comes back faster afterwards.

A vegetable garden and orchard provide much of the family's fresh food needs. Meat comes off the farm and milk from the Jersey cow, Tilly. Sarah calculated how much she was spending on milk for the family and decided keeping a cow was cheaper, as well as feeding a couple of fattening calves on any over-supply. Apart from cost, the fresh milk has another upside in that Sarah was having digestive problems after Isla's birth, which cleared up after she started on the raw milk. Sarah maintains that the children are healthier, too.

Sarah generally cooks for seven hungry mouths every night – 'there are never any leftovers!' She shops online, which saves time when she picks up her order once a week in Masterton, instead of trailing around the supermarket with the children. 'I just improvise when I run out of things – it's surprising what you have in the pantry.'

The couple has tentatively looked at properties back over the hill in easier country, but at this stage they love their rugged hills and coast too much. It might be a safe bet that if they do decide to change farms it'll be across the Cook Strait and somewhere down in the mainland mountains!

Lemon Cake

With two young children, Sarah looks for ways to cut corners to save both time and effort when cooking. Using a food processor to prepare this cake batter helps Sarah on both counts.

Prep time: *15 minutes*
Cook time: *35–45 minutes*
Makes: *20cm cake*

1¾ cups sugar
grated rind of 2 lemons
3 tablespoons lemon juice
2 eggs
1 cup light-flavoured oil
1 cup plain unsweetened yoghurt
2 cups self-raising flour

Topping
2 tablespoons lemon juice
2 tablespoons sugar

Preheat the oven to 180°C (160°C fan bake). Set the rack in the centre of the oven. Grease the base and sides of a 20cm square or round cake tin and line the base with baking paper.

In the bowl of a food processor fitted with the metal blade, put the sugar, lemon rind and juice and process to mix well. Add the eggs, oil and yoghurt and process until smooth. Sift the flour evenly into the food processor. Pulse to just mix. Transfer to the prepared tin.

Bake in the preheated oven for 35–45 minutes or until a skewer inserted into the centre comes out clean.

For the topping, brush the hot cake with the extra lemon juice and sprinkle with sugar. Leave in the tin to cool for 15–20 minutes before turning out onto a cake rack.

Welsh Brownie

A delightful, not-too-rich chocolate brownie that's ideal for the kids' lunchboxes or served warm with ice cream for dessert.

Prep time: *20 minutes*
Cook time: *30 minutes*
Makes: *16 pieces*

150 grams dark chocolate, chopped
100 grams butter
3 eggs, at room temperature
¾ cup soft brown sugar
1 teaspoon vanilla essence
¾ cup self-raising flour
⅓ cup sultanas

Preheat the oven to 180°C (160°C fan bake). Set the rack in the centre of the oven. Grease and line the base and sides of a 20cm square cake or slice tin.

Melt the dark chocolate and butter together, either in the microwave or in the top of a double saucepan. Set aside to cool.

Using an electric beater, beat the eggs, sugar and vanilla essence until thick and frothy. Stir in the cooled chocolate and butter and fold in the flour and sultanas. Transfer to the prepared tin and spread out evenly.

Bake in the preheated oven for 30 minutes. Do not over-bake; the brownie should be slightly soft in the centre.

Leave to cool before dusting with icing sugar and slicing into pieces.

Stored in an airtight container, these brownies will keep for 7–10 days.

FAMILY
RULES
Help each other
BE THANKFUL
Know you are loved
Pay with hugs and kisses
Try new things
BE HAPPY
Show compassion
BE GRATEFUL
DREAM BIG
Respect one another
LAUGH OUT LOUD
SAY I LOVE YOU

Parlies (Scottish Parliament Cakes)

These simple cakes, a favourite of Sarah's, have a rather colourful history. In F. Marian McNeill's respected book *The Scots Kitchen*, parlies are said to be a kind of gingerbread cake, popular with the members of parliament. It also suggests that these cakes were baked by a generous lady who seemingly offered more than her freshly baked parlies to male customers! More ginger may be added to suit your taste.

Prep time: *15 minutes*
Cook time: *15–20 minutes*
Makes: *16 cakes*

125 grams butter, softened
¼ cup sugar
2 tablespoons golden syrup or treacle (originally black treacle was used)
1 egg, beaten
1¾ cups flour
1 teaspoon ground ginger

Preheat the oven to 180°C. Set the rack in the centre of the oven or, if using two baking trays, place a rack either side of the centre to ensure even cooking. Grease 1–2 baking trays.

Beat the butter and sugar together until creamy. Add the golden syrup or treacle and egg and beat well. Sift the flour and ginger together and stir into the creamed mixture. Drop dessertspoonfuls onto the prepared tray/s, leaving room for the parlies to spread.

Bake in the preheated oven for 15–20 minutes or until firm to the touch. Transfer to a cake rack to cool.

Once cool, store in an airtight container for up to 2 weeks. The ginger flavour will become more pronounced over time.

Ethel's Gingerbread

In times past, ginger was one of the first spices readily available to cook with, so many families had their own unique gingerbread recipes. The treacle or golden syrup gave the bread a rich flavour and kept it moist. This recipe, full of flavour and delicious with a slice of Cheddar-style cheese, can be traced back some decades to family in northern Ireland.

Prep time: *20 minutes*
Cook time: *1½ hours*
Makes: *1 large loaf*

500 grams flour
1½ teaspoons ground ginger
2 teaspoons baking powder
½ teaspoon baking soda
½ teaspoon salt
1¼ cups soft brown sugar
175 grams butter
375 grams treacle or golden syrup, or a blend of both
1¼ cups milk
1 egg, beaten

Preheat the oven to 180°C (160°C fan bake). Set the rack in or just below the centre of the oven. Grease the base and sides of a large (21cm x 11cm) loaf tin and line the base and sides with baking paper.

Sift the flour, ginger, baking powder, baking soda and salt into a large bowl. Stir in the brown sugar and make a well in the centre.

Melt the butter in a saucepan over a low heat. Stir in the treacle or golden syrup and just warm through. Pour into the well with the milk and egg. Using a wooden spoon, beat well to make a smooth batter. Pour into the prepared tin.

Bake in the preheated oven for 1½ hours or until a skewer inserted into the centre of the loaf comes out clean. Cool in the tin for 30 minutes before turning out onto a cake rack to cool completely.

The flavour of the gingerbread will be enhanced if it is kept in an airtight tin for a few days before slicing. If kept in a tightly lidded container away from heat and light, gingerbread will keep for 3 weeks or more.

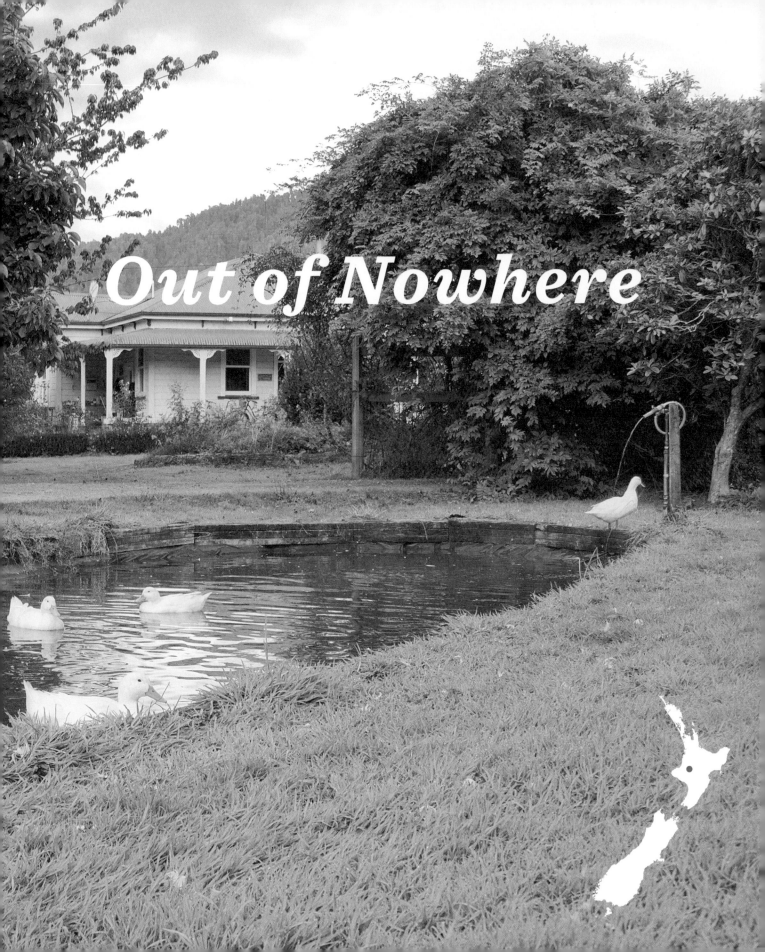

Out of Nowhere

'We're in the middle of nowhere!' the holidaying German biker addressed all and sundry in the Blue Duck Café.

'No, it's the beginning of everywhere,' responded Blue Duck's owner, Dan Steele. Standing on a clear, pitch-black night beneath a vast, star-carpeted sky, the only sounds the river, kiwi and the occasional roar from a stag, you feel he may well be right – this is a very special place.

Dan, farmer, Massey University alumnus, husband, father, ardent conservationist, environmentalist and 2015 Nuffield Farming Scholar, inspires optimism about the future of this country. His 3700 acres – half in bush – lie on the confluence of the Whanganui and Retaruke rivers, some 42 kilometres off SH4 south of Taumarunui. Much of the road is twisty and unsealed, flanked by evidence of slips that indicate the heavy rainfall and fragile nature of the land.

His farm is Whakahoro; over a suspension bridge across the river is his parents' property, Retaruke Station. Leading from the café, a roadway – built by Irish navvies as access to the ill-fated Mangapurua settlement – is a gateway to Whanganui National Park and a network of walks and cycle paths. Drainage off the bush-clad hills is via tunnels carved into the rock, which contain a treasure trove of insects, including giant weta. This is all part and parcel of Dan's vision for conservation of this country, which also boasts a large population of kiwi and dwindling numbers of whio (blue duck). Dan is determined to halt the whio's decline and build up numbers. Whakahoro, which has gradually expanded as Dan has bought other parcels of land, carries 500 Angus/Belted Galloway/Hereford-cross cattle and 3000 Romney/Perendale-cross sheep. Blue Duck Station encompasses the whole area.

Dan and his wife Sandy live in one of the old homesteads on the property with son Blue (4) and daughter Snow (1). Sandy, originally from Coromandel, owns Snowy Waters Lodge in Raetihi. The couple founded and are trustees of the Whanganui National Park Conservation and Historic Preservation Trust.

Dan's a hunter–gatherer sort of guy, as are several of the similarly impassioned and inspiring young people – eight staff members and varying numbers of 'eco-warrior' volunteers – with whom he has surrounded himself in the businesses of farming, conservation and tourism. The volunteers help maintain the lodges, work in the vegetable garden and, importantly, help lay and service traplines in the bush to rid it of rats, possums, stoats and feral cats.

Blue Duck Station attracts visitors – 200 a week in high season – with a bent for adventure: horse trekking, kayaking, jet boating, hunting, claybird shooting, tramping, mountain biking, bush safaris. Dan calculates that they now accommodate 13,000 bed nights a year in comfortable self-catering lodges; many of the visitors disgorge from Stray's buses on a regular basis. Meals are available in the Blue Duck Café, where the chef cooks from the large vegetable garden and utilises home-grown meats as well as goat, rabbit, venison and pork all shot on the farm – nothing could be fresher. Blue Duck manuka honey comes from a multitude of busy hives.

Dan's mother and father, Rachel and Richard, first-generation farmers with a passion for flora and fauna, came here from the western shores of Lake Taupo with Dan and brother Rich, who is Dan's 'Mr Fixit' contractor but works full time on Retaruke. Dan's sister Anna is an accountant.

Richard and Rachel have lived for over 20 years in the original 105-year-old homestead, Granville House, built by English immigrant James Sarsfield Lacy, overlooking the river. Here Rachel has her beloved garden, overflowing with vegetables and herbs, of which she has 35 different varieties, and the orchard provides fruit.

Rachel is a keen cook and, while the kitchen is modern, she says, 'My favourite cooking utensils are a bowl and a wooden spoon.' Richard says that he feels privileged. 'I am married to the best cook in New Zealand.' Rachel is also a keen quilter and collector of quilts old and new.

Last word to Dan: 'This [Blue Duck Station] is my source of inspiration; spirituality to me is Mother Nature. Our environment is the most valuable and important asset we have.'

Retaruke Gingernuts

These gingernuts bake to perfection – crunchy and moreish. The original recipe, amended by Rachel to include baking powder, came from the *Listener*'s award-winning – now retired – food writer Lois Daish.

Prep time: *30 minutes*
Cook time: *18–20 minutes*
Makes: *about 36 gingernuts*

100 grams butter
1 cup caster sugar
1 egg
1 tablespoon golden syrup
2 cups flour
1 teaspoon baking soda
1 teaspoon baking powder
3–4 teaspoons ground ginger

Preheat the oven to 170°C (150°C fan bake). Set the rack in the centre of the oven or, if using two baking trays, place a rack either side of the centre to ensure even cooking. Grease 1–2 baking trays or line with baking paper.

Cream the butter and sugar until light and fluffy. Add the egg and golden syrup and mix well.

In a separate bowl, sift the flour, baking soda, baking powder and ginger. Add to the creamed mixture and combine well. Roll generous teaspoonfuls of mixture into balls and place on the prepared tray/s, leaving room for the biscuits to spread. Do not press the biscuits down; they will spread out into even rounds as they cook.

Bake in the preheated oven for 18–20 minutes or until the biscuits are cracked on top and are a deep ginger-brown colour. Cool on the tray/s until firm and then transfer to a cake rack to cool completely.

If stored in an airtight container away from heat and light, these gingernuts will keep well for 2–3 weeks.

COOK'S TIP
- If you don't have a cup measure, weigh the flour. For the recipes in this book, 1 cup flour is equal to 125 grams.

Rachel's Amish Apple Cake

This sweetly spiced apple cake with a nutty streusel topping is easy and quick to make, and it uses pantry staples. Adapt the recipe to suit what you have at hand; the apples can be exchanged for pears or peaches, almonds or pecans can be used in place of the walnuts, and nutmeg, mace or mixed spice are good alternatives to the cinnamon.

Prep time: *30 minutes*
Cook time: *35–45 minutes*
Makes: *23cm cake*

1½ cups flour
1 teaspoon baking powder
1 teaspoon baking soda
½ teaspoon salt
1 rounded cup sugar
⅓ cup milk
75 grams butter, melted
1 egg, beaten
3 cups peeled, diced apple

Topping
1 cup walnuts, chopped
1 cup soft brown sugar
1 tablespoon flour
2 teaspoons ground cinnamon
50 grams butter, melted

Preheat the oven to 180°C (160°C fan bake). Set the rack in the centre of the oven. Grease the base and sides of a 23cm square cake tin (or one of similar size) and line with baking paper.

In a large bowl, sift together the flour, baking powder, baking soda and salt. Stir in the sugar and make a well in the centre. Into the well, put the milk, butter, egg and apple and mix gently, just until all the ingredients are combined. Transfer to the prepared tin.

To make the topping, put the walnuts, brown sugar, flour, cinnamon and butter into a separate bowl and use a fork to make a crumble-like mix. Scatter over the cake batter.

Bake in the preheated oven for 35–45 minutes or until a skewer inserted into the centre comes out clean. Cool in the tin.

Stored in an airtight container, this cake will keep for 5–7 days.

Serve the cake on its own, or accompanied with custard for a dessert.

Rosemary's 'No Knead' Bread

There's no bread machine required to make this moist, light-textured wholemeal bread which, given it's over an hour to the closest shop, Rachel prepares weekly for her family.

Prep time: *30 minutes*

Rising time: *1 hour*

Cook time: *1–1¼ hours*

Makes: *3 loaves*

6–7 cups lukewarm water
4 teaspoons sugar
4 teaspoons active dried yeast
8 cups wholemeal flour
4 cups flour
5 teaspoons salt
about 1 cup sunflower or pumpkin seeds, optional

Grease three medium-sized (22cm x 9cm) loaf tins.

In a large jug, stir together 6 cups of the water with the sugar and yeast and leave for 10 minutes or until a yeasty froth has appeared on top of the water.

In a large bowl, stir together the flours and salt. Stir in the sunflower or pumpkin seeds, if using, and make a well in the centre. Gradually pour in the yeast mixture, stirring with a wooden spoon. Add the remaining water, if required, to make a sticky dough. Divide the mixture evenly among the prepared tins, and set aside in a warm place for about 1 hour, or until the dough has risen almost to the top of the tins.

While the dough is rising, preheat the oven to 190°C (170°C fan bake).

If wished, just before baking, sprinkle a few extra sunflower or pumpkin seeds on top of the loaves. Bake in the preheated oven for 1–1¼ hours, or until the bread sounds hollow when tapped. Transfer immediately to a cake rack to cool.

This bread can be stored in a bread tin and used within the week. It freezes well.

Serve sliced with butter or soft cheeses, or toasted and well buttered.

COOK'S TIP
• For this recipe use standard dried yeast granules.

An Unexpected Inheritance

'It hadn't been lived in for about five years when we moved to Gisborne. We had to make the decision whether to set a match to it or spend some serious money on it; otherwise we would have lost it. None of the toilets worked! The bones were still pretty good, but water had started getting in.'

Dan Russell is talking about the 110-year-old homestead at Puketiti Station, inland from Te Puia Springs on the East Coast. The homestead was built in 1906 by A. B. Williams, largely with Oregon pine, carried as ballast in wool ships, and native timber panelling. A. B.'s brother, H. B. Williams, settled on Turihaua (see page 130), closer to Gisborne.

Dan grew up the youngest of three brothers on Tuna Nui Station (see page 146), in Hawke's Bay, but chose flying as his career. Completely out of the blue, when he was 27, he inherited Puketiti from his uncle and godfather, Des Williams, who died in 1997. Fortunately, Des realised the impact of the bequest and had put in place a trust to run the place for seven years, giving Dan, and subsequently his wife Anna, time to make a decision. In 2004, Dan took up the responsibility of Puketiti, though no one was more aware than he of his shortcomings as a landowner and farmer!

'I'm the odd job man . . . yesterday it was IT and plumbing . . . jack of all trades and master of none,' he says deprecatingly.

A team of a manager, two shepherds and a fencer/general hand tends to the day-to-day farming of the Angus cattle herd and Romney sheep run on the property. Some 700 acres of forestry is in Dan's portfolio. There is also a 70-acre redwood forest planted four years ago as a carbon sink project. Anna, an ex-Aucklander, took readily to the remote rural life and now manages the station accounts.

The couple's focus is on maintaining the Category 1 historic homestead, along with the old stables and woolshed – the oldest building on the station – and the extensive gardens and 30-acre arboretum established in 1915.

They have not done a lot to the house 'other than repairs and painting'; their priority is restoration as opposed to renovation. However, when the *Country Calendar Homestead Baking* team were there, Anna was preparing for the imminent modernising of the kitchen to be more convenient, yet retaining its character.

Initially, they found the house 'freezing', so the first priority was a new roof, replacing rotten weatherboards and repainting the exterior. That was an expensive and major exercise on an eight-bedroom house with extensive public rooms, built at the turn of the century for a much larger family with live-in staff! A wall between the kitchen – heated by a Falcon range – and a former maid's sitting room was removed to open out the area and provide a family room and office leading to the rear verandah. Recently a sprinkler system was installed, providing peace of mind.

The billiard room, with its eight-legged table, has an elaborately panelled ceiling and an even more ornate totara fire surround, carved by A. B. Williams' niece, artist Ruth Nelson, in the 1930s. It's a great room for social gatherings.

In the dining room, there's a solid black maire dining table made by the station carpenter. In past times, the head of the table could press a bell with his foot to summon the servants! A sweeping staircase leads to the upper-floor bedrooms and bathrooms, with a narrower version off the kitchen for the servants. Other treasures include beautiful china and silver from Tuna Nui.

In the spirit of Dan's forebears, who were recognised for their philanthropy, Puketiti supports numerous local organisations, including rugby, netball and the 'local' junior All Blacks. With Puketiti a focal point for social occasions, Dan and Anna encourage a sense of community with the locals – some of whom work on a casual basis on the station at peak times. Friends of the couple were married in a grove in the garden, known as 'the cathedral', with a sit-down dinner afterwards for 75 in the original workshop and stables building.

Dan carries the tradition of service further: he is involved with SurfAid, an international charity founded in 2000 by three Gisborne surfing enthusiasts, two doctors and a lawyer. It provides health aid, particularly to mothers and children, in the remote Mentawai Islands of Sumatra and in parts of Indonesia.

Dan regards the East Coast as 'a special place'. He feels privileged to be the guardian of Puketiti and is very aware of caring for the land in the most environmentally sustainable way.

As the sun rises each day, it first strikes Mt Hikurangi and next lights up the hills and valleys of the 7000-acre (2833-hectare) station. It seems an auspicious omen for the future of the historic property.

Aunt Anne's Scones

When we arrived at Puketiti, Anna had prepared for us slow-roasted mutton with caramelised onion. Mutton is well-favoured by farming communities, but sadly neglected today by many city folk, a trend which deserves reversing. Anna shredded the leftovers and shredded them down to add to her favourite scone recipe, a creation of Anna's Aunt Anne, who would never waste a morsel. In place of mutton, you could use lamb, beef or venison.

Prep time: *10 minutes*
Cook time: *10–12 minutes*
Makes: *12–14 scones*

2 cups flour
4 teaspoons baking powder
2 eggs, beaten

2 cups pulled mutton and caramelised onion (or use grated cheese or chopped dates)
milk to bind

Preheat the oven to 190°C (170°C fan bake). Set the rack just above the centre of the oven. Grease a baking tray.

Sift the flour and baking powder into a large bowl and make a well in the centre. Stir through the beaten eggs, pulled mutton and onion or filling of your choice, and add sufficient milk to bind to a soft, spoonable scone dough. Place large spoonfuls on the prepared tray.

Bake in the preheated oven for 10–12 minutes or until the scones are golden brown and cooked. Transfer to a clean, cloth-covered cake rack or basket and serve warm.

Phillida's Oat Biscuits

These chewy oat biscuits from Dan's mother Phillida, with their overload of butter and sweet warmth from the golden syrup, are very hard to beat.

Prep time: *10 minutes*
Cook time: *25–30 minutes*
Makes: *20 biscuits*

4 cups rolled oats
1 cup sugar

250 grams butter
3 tablespoons golden syrup

Preheat the oven to 180°C (160°C fan bake). Set the rack just below the centre of the oven. Grease the base and sides of a 20cm x 30cm slice tin and line the base with baking paper.

Put the oats and sugar in a large bowl and stir together.

Melt the butter and golden syrup together. Pour into the oat mixture and stir together to make a buttery crumb-like mix. Press into the prepared slice tin.

Bake in the preheated oven for 25–30 minutes until toasty brown in colour.

Remove from the oven and mark into pieces with a knife while hot. Cool in the tin before turning out and cutting into pieces.

Stored in an airtight container, these biscuits will keep well for 2–3 weeks.

Aunt Anne's Scones

Phillida's Oat Biscuits

Maureen's Easy Carrot Cake

This cake is very easy to make, not too sweet and rather delicious.

Prep time: *20 minutes*
Cook time: *1½ hours*
Makes: *25cm cake*

5 eggs, at room temperature
1¾ cups sugar
1½ cups light-flavoured oil
3 cups grated carrot
1 cup chopped walnuts
1 cup raisins or sultanas
2 cups flour
2 teaspoons ground cinnamon
1 quantity Lemon Cream Cheese Icing (see recipe on page 265)
pumpkin seeds, dried cranberries and dried apricots
  for decorating, optional

Preheat the oven to 170°C (150°C fan bake). Set the rack in the centre of the oven. Grease the base and sides of a 25cm square cake tin (or similar), and line the base with baking paper.

In a large bowl, stir together the eggs and sugar until the mixture has become a liquid-like consistency. Stir in the oil, carrot, walnuts and raisins or sultanas. Sift the flour and cinnamon together and stir into the egg mixture. Mix well. Transfer to the prepared cake tin.

Bake in the preheated oven for 1½ hours. Check after 1 hour and, if the top of the cake is browning too much, cover with a piece of baking paper. Continue to cook until a skewer inserted into the centre of the cake comes out clean. Leave to stand in the cake tin for 15 minutes before turning out onto a cake rack to cool completely.

When cold, ice with lemon cream cheese icing and, if wished, decorate with the pumpkin seeds, dried cranberries and dried apricots.

Store in an airtight container in a cool place. Alternatively, keep the cake in the refrigerator – especially over summer. This cake is best eaten within a week.

Sarah's Gin and Tonic Cake

What a wonderful flavour combination. Serve this cake in the cool of a lazy hot summer's afternoon, accompanied with the eponymous drink!

Prep time: *30 minutes*

Cook time: *45–50 minutes*

Makes: *20cm cake*

250 grams butter, softened
1 cup caster sugar
4 eggs, at room temperature
½ cup gin
grated rind and juice of 2 lemons
2 cups self-raising flour, sifted

Gin Glaze
½ cup caster sugar
⅓–½ cup gin
dash of tonic
finely shredded rind and juice of 1 lemon
2 kaffir lime leaves, finely shredded, optional

Preheat the oven to 170–180°C (150–160°C fan bake). Set the rack in the centre of the oven. Grease the base and sides of a 20cm square cake tin and line the base with baking paper.

Beat the butter and sugar together until pale cream in colour and fluffy in texture. This will take a good 10 minutes. Add the eggs one at a time, beating well after each addition.

Mix the gin, lemon rind and juice together. Fold the sifted flour into the creamed mixture alternately with the gin and lemon mixture. Transfer to the prepared cake tin.

Bake in the preheated oven for 45–50 minutes or until a skewer inserted into the centre comes out clean. Remove from the oven and leave the cake to cool in the tin while making the glaze.

To make the glaze, in a saucepan over a low heat, stir together all the gin glaze ingredients until the sugar has dissolved. Slowly pour the glaze over the cake.

Serve warm or cold, with whipped cream to accompany. Stored in an airtight container, this cake will keep well for 7–10 days.

Heather's Delight

The mother of one of Anna's oldest friends gave Anna the recipe for this crunchy cereal-based variation on the classic caramel slice, complete with the much-loved condensed milk caramel filling and, just for good measure, a thick layer of dark chocolate – scandalously rich but ever so good!

Prep time: *15 minutes*
Cook time: *20–22 minutes*
Makes: *20–24 pieces*

Base
2 cups flour
2 teaspoons cocoa
1 teaspoon baking powder
1 cup soft brown sugar
1 cup Coco Pops
250 grams butter, melted
1 teaspoon vanilla essence or extract

Caramel Filling
395-gram can sweetened condensed milk
2 tablespoons golden syrup
25 grams butter

Chocolate Topping
200 grams dark chocolate, chopped

Preheat the oven to 180°C (160°C fan bake). Set the rack in the centre of the oven. Grease the base and sides of a 20cm x 30cm slice tin and line the base with baking paper.

To make the base, sift the flour, cocoa and baking powder into a large bowl. Stir in the sugar and Coco Pops and make a well in the centre. Pour in the butter and vanilla and mix together. Press into the prepared slice tin.

Bake in the preheated oven for 10–12 minutes or until just firm to the touch.

While the base is cooking, prepare the caramel filling. In a saucepan over a moderate heat, heat the condensed milk, golden syrup and butter, stirring constantly until the mixture turns a golden caramel colour. Do not cook over a high heat as the mixture will burn quickly. Pour over the cooked base and spread out evenly. Return it to the oven for a further 10 minutes.

Remove from the oven and set aside to cool.

When cold, melt the dark chocolate, either in the microwave or in the top of a double saucepan, and spread evenly over the caramel. Allow the slice to become completely cold before cutting it into pieces.

Store in an airtight container. This moist slice will keep for 7–10 days.

Changing the Guard

One gets the feeling that the chaos in the homestead kitchen of the 2000-hectare Turihaua Station, just north of Gisborne, is nothing out of the ordinary. It's 'smoko' time and Angela Williams is flying to put tea, coffee and baking on the table. Today, gathered noisily and happily, are Angela and her husband Hamish; sons Paul and Toby with their wives Sarah and Amelia; daughter Belinda (who lives in town); grandchildren Jackson (3), Ruby (3), Max (2) and Hugo (1) (Tristan, aged 7, arrives later in the day after school); Diane Moore, a long-time friend of the family; farm staff Nick, Danny and Harry, and Nick's wife, Hine. Add the *Country Calendar Homestead Baking* team and it's just as well that the kitchen, dining area and family room are spacious. 'It's always like a railway station with people,' Angela laughs. The Williams family has farmed Turihaua since the 1800s and now the fifth generation is firmly in the driving seat. The station is noted for its outstanding Turihaua Angus stud, founded in 1906. Twice a year buyers flock to purchase pedigree bulls (and top heifers) at sales in the farm's own complex, while an expanding enterprise is in the sale of semen and embryos to overseas breeders. There have always been two arms to the farm – the pedigree herd and the commercial herd for beef production. Of the 2000 hectares, 1800 are actively farmed, with the remainder in forestry or retired under the QEII Trust.

Hamish and Angela are looking towards retirement and succession plans are already in action, with the farm now in two divisions. Toby manages the commercial business, which focuses on beef and lambs, and Paul is stud stock manager. Hamish is still boss but is steering more from the back seat, taking an overall view of the new regime and letting his sons make the decisions. He is a strong believer in having a sustainable farming system and 'letting the environment tell us what to do'.

Outstanding quality is the watchword in everything the farm produces, and all stock is recorded and tested. Angela maintains all the stud records. The best Turihaua beef and lamb are sold through the Gisborne Deli & Butchery. The cattle are trucked to Ruakura, rested there for several weeks and then walked in from the paddock to the abattoir, eliminating stress.

Beef also goes to Angus Pure, while the Romney-cross lambs go to the Ovation abattoir in Gisborne.

The homestead was built by H. B. Williams, Hamish's grandfather, around 1913, with a second storey added in 1914. In 1920, it was altered by the same architect who had built the Puketiti homestead further north (see page 116). Hamish's parents did considerable alterations over 25 years of residence. The major change during the 30 years it has been home to Hamish and Angela has been to the kitchen–living area, which was originally two rooms. The windows at the front of the house open over colourful gardens to the spectacular coastline over the main road, through a protective barrier of tall trees. Fantails dance on the lawn, white doves perch on a chimney and an imposing palm soars outside the front door.

The formal dining room is overlooked by portraits of family forebears and there are photos throughout the house of the family through the generations. A big billiard room also suggests lots of parties; the Williams do a lot of entertaining. Angela says, 'It has always been a home open to others,' and adds that her mother-in-law, Elizabeth ('Marnie'), was 'a great hostess'. The formal sitting room looks over the extensive lawn. A couple of the seven bedrooms were maids' quarters in times past, and there are five bathrooms. In the 1960s much of the timber upstairs was painted over, but luckily the heart rimu downstairs remains natural.

A vegetable and berry garden that 'grows most things' is Angela's fiefdom. Her hens provide eggs, and a prolific orchard produces apricots, peaches, mandarins, apples, lemons, persimmons, quinces and feijoas, all of which mean an annual fever of bottling and preserving. A very old grapevine winds around the bottom storey of the house. Angela enjoys cooking, especially beef and lamb: 'We do home-kill lamb for the house, but not many cattle.' Instead, local butcher Darryn Clyne cuts a beast up and vacuum-packs it for Angela to freeze. It's a busy, busy life on which Angela thrives: 'You can be Supermum – that's good – but don't try to be Superwoman!'

Turihaua may revolve around its outstanding stock, but it is also about family, and its heart is Angela's homestead kitchen. She delights in having her sons, daughters-in-law and grandchildren around every day, with her daughter just along the road. 'Not many people have that.'

Chocolate Fudge Slice

No-bake slices are popular at Turihaua as they are easy to make and keep well. This decadent fudge-like slice is prepared from a classic ganache, or chocolate cream. It is very rich and very moreish!

Prep time: *30 minutes*

Chill time: *3–4 hours*

Makes: *about 30 pieces*

Chocolate Cream
2 cups cream
500 grams dark chocolate, chopped
1 teaspoon vanilla essence or extract

Biscuit Mix
250 grams plain sweet biscuits, crushed

¾ cup desiccated coconut
2 cups chopped dried fruit (dried cranberries, blueberries, raisins or apricots)
1 cup roughly chopped nuts (pistachios, walnuts, almonds)
¼ cup chopped dark chocolate (or use chocolate chips)
100 grams white chocolate

Line the base and sides of a 20cm x 26cm slice tin with baking paper.

In a saucepan over a moderate heat, bring the cream to scalding point (just before boiling), then remove from the heat. Stir in the dark chocolate and vanilla and continue to stir until the chocolate has melted.

In a large bowl, toss together the biscuit crumbs, coconut, dried fruit, nuts and chopped chocolate. Add sufficient chocolate cream to combine all the ingredients (reserve the remainder for the icing). The amount required will vary depending on the brand of biscuits used and how finely they are crushed. Press the mixture firmly into the tin. Spread the remaining chocolate cream over the slice and refrigerate for 3–4 hours or until firm.

Melt the white chocolate in the microwave, using only a moderate heat, as white chocolate will overheat quickly and seize. Pipe or drizzle over the slice to decorate. When the slice is set, cut into pieces to serve.

Stored in the refrigerator, this slice will keep well for 2–3 weeks. However, to really appreciate the rich chocolate taste, remove from the refrigerator 30 minutes before serving.

COOK'S TIP
• To crush the biscuits, place them in a sealable plastic bag and roll firmly with a rolling pin. Alternatively, pulse them in a food processor.

Apricot and Coconut Slice

Dried New Zealand apricots will provide the best flavour for this slice. If planning to serve this to adults, soak the apricots in a dash of brandy or Grand Marnier beforehand.

Prep time: *15 minutes*

Chill time: *3–4 hours*

Makes: *about 30 pieces*

100 grams butter, diced
½ x 395-gram can sweetened condensed milk
250-gram packet plain sweet biscuits, crushed
1 cup finely chopped dried apricots
1 cup desiccated coconut
½ cup chopped almonds
¼ cup lemon juice

Icing
3½ cups icing sugar
50 grams butter, melted
1 teaspoon lemon juice
about 3 tablespoons boiling water
½ cup flaked almonds, toasted
grated rind of 1 lemon

Line a 20cm x 26cm slice tin with baking paper.

Put the butter and condensed milk into a saucepan over a low heat and cook for 2 minutes, stirring all the time until the butter has melted and the mixture is hot. Stir in the biscuits, apricots, coconut, almonds and lemon juice. If the mixture is a little dry, add extra condensed milk a tablespoon at a time until a sticky, thick texture is reached. Press into the prepared tin and refrigerate for 1 hour.

To make the icing, sift the icing sugar into a bowl and stir in the butter and lemon juice with sufficient boiling water to make a thick, spreadable icing. Spread over the chilled slice. Scatter over the almonds and grated lemon rind.

Refrigerate for 2–3 hours or until firm. Cut into squares.

Stored in an airtight container in the refrigerator, this slice will keep well for 2–3 weeks.

Sponge Drops

There is not a party held at Turihaua that Angela does not prepare these classic, simply delicious goodies. The recipe has been passed down three generations and, given its popularity with the grandchildren, looks likely to continue on to the next generation. In the days before spring or digital scales and cup measurements, people used balance scales, and eggs were used as the base weight to measure the other ingredients such as flour, butter and sugar – hence the measurements in this recipe.

Prep time: *20 minutes*

Cook time: *10–12 minutes*

Makes: *about 20 sandwiched sponge drops*

3 eggs, at room temperature
caster sugar
flour
1 teaspoon baking powder

Cream Filling
300ml bottle cream, chilled
2 tablespoons icing sugar
2–3 drops vanilla essence or extract

Preheat the oven to 170°C (150°C fan bake). Set the rack in the centre of the oven or, if using two baking trays, place a rack either side of the centre to ensure even cooking. Grease 1–2 baking trays and dust with flour or line with baking paper.

Weigh the eggs and take note of the weight. Measure **three** times the weight of the eggs in sugar, then measure **two** times the weight of the eggs in flour.

Sift the flour and baking powder together.

In a clean bowl, whisk the eggs until frothy and light. Add the sugar and beat for at least 10 minutes until very thick. Fold in the sifted flour. Place spoonfuls of the mixture onto the prepared tray/s, leaving room for the sponge drops to spread. Use a teaspoon for small sponge drops and a tablespoon for larger sponge drops.

Bake in the preheated oven for 10–12 minutes, or until the drops are firm to the touch in the centre and lightly brown in colour. Transfer to a cake rack to cool.

Store in an airtight container until ready to fill and serve. The unfilled sponge drops will keep for about 4–5 days.

Whip the cream, icing sugar and vanilla together until the mixture becomes thick and forms soft peaks. Refrigerate until required.

To serve, sandwich two similar-sized sponge drops with whipped cream. Set aside, in a single layer, in the refrigerator or a very cool place for 2–4 hours to ensure the sponge drops soften before serving. Dust with icing sugar before arranging on a plate to serve.

Pavlova Roll with Lemon Filling

In her book *The Pavlova Story*, professor Helen Leach from Otago University tells us that the Pavlova Roll arrived here with our Aussie cousins in the 1980s, after it appeared in a cookbook from Meedo Station, Western Australia – though given their penchant for claiming what's ours as theirs, there may be, says Helen, a longer story behind the evolution of the Pavlova Roll. At Turihau, Angela deftly whipped up this pavlova roll for us in minutes. She likes to fill the centre with her home-made lemon honey and sweetened whipped cream.

Prep time: *30 minutes*

Chill time: *2–3 hours*

Cook time: *30 minutes (15 minutes each for the lemon filling and pavlova)*

Serves: *8–10*

Lemon Honey
4 egg yolks
½ cup sugar
grated rind and juice of 1 lemon
juice of 1 orange

Pavlova
4 egg whites
½ cup caster sugar
2 teaspoons vinegar
1 teaspoon cornflour
½ cup flaked almonds or desiccated coconut
300ml bottle cream, chilled and whipped

To make the lemon honey, mix together the egg yolks, sugar, lemon rind and juice and orange juice in the top of a double saucepan or a heatproof bowl. Sit above a saucepan of simmering water and heat, stirring constantly, until the lemon mixture begins to thicken. Do not rush the process or the eggs will scramble. Once the mixture is thick enough to coat the back of a wooden spoon, remove from the heat, transfer to a bowl, and cover the surface of the lemon honey with plastic wrap – this prevents a skin forming. Refrigerate for a minimum of 2–3 hours until chilled.

Preheat the oven to 180°C (160°C fan bake). Set the rack in the centre of the oven. Line and then grease a 26cm x 36cm sponge roll tin or one of similar size.

In a scrupulously clean bowl, whip the egg whites until frothy and thick. Gradually beat in the sugar until the mixture becomes very thick and glossy. Quickly beat in the vinegar and cornflour. Spread the mixture evenly into the prepared tin. Sprinkle with the flaked almonds or coconut.

Bake in the preheated oven for 15 minutes until the pavlova is golden brown on top and feels 'set' to the touch. While baking, cut a piece of baking paper that is large enough to hold the pavlova, place on a bench and sprinkle lightly with caster sugar.

Once the pavlova is cooked, remove from the oven. Carefully turn over onto the sugared baking paper and remove the baking paper lining from the pavlova base. Cool for 2–3 minutes. Spread a layer of lemon filling on top, and then a layer of whipped cream. Using the baking paper as a guide, roll the long side over to enclose the filling. Carefully transfer the roll to a large platter to serve. The pavlova roll can be refrigerated for 2–4 hours before serving.

Marnie's Date and Nut Cake with Coconut Topping

As this is the cake that is most requested by the farmhands, Angela usually doubles the recipe – which is from her mother-in-law Marnie – baking it in a 24cm cake tin. On the day of our visit, we enjoyed the cake with a caramel sauce (see page 265) – a delightful partner to this date cake. Custard or vanilla-scented pouring cream would also be delicious.

Prep time: *30 minutes*
Cook time: *60 minutes*
Makes: *20cm cake*

1 cup chopped dates
1 cup boiling water
1 teaspoon baking soda
125 grams butter, softened
1 cup sugar
1 egg, at room temperature, beaten
1½ cups flour, sifted
½ cup chopped walnuts or almonds

Topping
75 grams butter
2 tablespoons milk
½ cup soft brown sugar
1 cup desiccated coconut

Preheat the oven to 160°C (140°C fan bake). Set the rack in the centre of the oven. Grease and line the base and sides of a 20cm loose-bottom cake tin, making sure the baking paper comes all the way up the sides of the tin.

Stir the dates, boiling water and soda together and allow to stand until lukewarm.

Beat the butter and sugar together until light and creamy. Add the egg and beat well. Gently stir in the date mixture, flour and nuts. Transfer to the prepared cake tin.

Bake in the preheated oven for 40–45 minutes or until a skewer inserted into the centre comes out clean.

While the cake is baking, prepare the topping. Bring the butter and milk to the boil in a small saucepan. Add the brown sugar and bring back to the boil. Remove from the heat and stir in the coconut.

When the cake is cooked, remove from the oven and pour the hot topping over the hot cake. Return to the oven for a further 10–12 minutes or until the topping is golden. Allow the cake to cool in the tin before transferring to a cake rack, taking care not to dislodge any of the topping.

This is delicious served warm as a dessert.

Upholding Tradition

TUNANUI

TRADE MARK
DONALDS
PATENT
MASTERTON N.Z.
No W

HOMESTEAD

The scene was straight from an English stately home – luxury cars and 4WDs parked alongside battered Land Rovers, muddy pick-ups and elderly saloons. Gentlemen in tweeds, Barbour jackets and cheesecutters; ladies in elegantly tailored wool suits, hose with flashed garters, fashionable but practical boots and tweed hats decorated with pheasant feathers. Children, ditto! A gamekeeper, suitably ruddy in complexion, and less fashionably clad beaters and pickers-up with excitedly panting Labradors and springer spaniels straining at their leashes complete the picture.

However, the backdrop, instead of being an ancestral castle, is the historic homestead of Tuna Nui Station in Hawke's Bay. The commercial pheasant shoots, run in conjunction with neighbours Jeff Niblett and Bridgette Karetai, make up just one element of a successful farming operation. All participants gather for refreshments and briefing in the original woolshed, built in 1878.

Under the guardianship of the Russell family since 1861, Tuna Nui homestead is presently home to the fifth and sixth generations: Andrew, Pip, Arthur (14) and Georgia (12); while Andrew's brother Sam, his wife Steph and two daughters and matriarch Phillida, who has an active involvement, all live elsewhere on the station. Sam is stock manager; Andrew has business interests off-farm and is the shoot manager. Tuna Nui carries 1000 beef cattle and 5500 sheep over two properties totalling 3500 acres (1416 hectares). The Russells have followed a biological system of farming for the past 7–8 years and have seen a marked improvement in animal health.

In 1895, WWI hero Major General Sir Andrew Russell KCB, KCMG, took over the running of his father's block, continually making improvements and caring for the property (with the aid of managers) until he died, aged 92, in 1960. The General's presence still looms large over Tuna Nui; in the homestead are many mementoes – including his helmet, shot through by a sniper – of his varied and full life. He continues to be something of a compass for the family. His grandson, John, took over in 1961, in turn handing over to Andrew and Sam in 1992.

The homestead, the second on the site, was commissioned by the General and his wife, Gertrude (daughter of J. N. Williams, founder of the Turihaua Angus stud – see page 130). The story goes that Gertrude's mother had indicated that the original house was not suitably grand for her daughter! In 1912–13, architect C. T. Natusch designed the house, with substantial input from Gertrude. Modern for the era, it stands on concrete foundations and piles. Most of the timber is native – the floors are rimu and matai, although cedar was used for windows, exterior doors and the slats holding the exterior roughcast. The Marseilles tiles were imported as ship's ballast. The house is cool in summer and very quiet, attributable to fine pumice which fills the internal walls – the Pink Batts of the time! The General planted most of the lovely old trees, and Gertrude designed and developed the spacious garden. Their successors John and Phillida carried on the good work over their 45 years in residence.

Now Andrew and Pip are the homestead's caretakers. Says Andrew, 'You don't live in a house like this unless you are slightly bonkers! You have to love the house and you have to have lived in it as a child.' He hopes that one of his children will live in it, love and care for it, but 'nothing is assumed'.

Not much has been changed, although the kitchen was renovated a few years ago, to open it out. 'Phillida spent 40 years up on tiptoe to look out of the window,' says her son. Upstairs, the bedrooms open out onto a terrace. Apart from one original old toilet, the bathrooms have been modernised; there's even a lift. Further up, under the roof, the attic houses family memorabilia; nobody knows exactly what is up there!

The house gets cold in winter, but the kitchen area is comfortably warm. It's also 'catering central' for the 20-plus shoots between May and August: Pip and friends prepare hearty soups, pheasant pies, hot hams and other goodies. Pip, who hails from Christchurch, learned cooking from her mother, grandmother and older sisters, and while she loves making risottos, roasts and one-dish meals, she confesses to being 'a bit rough in my baking!'

The dining room is original, and it delights Andrew and Pip that occasional shoot dinners in the homestead let them use the whole house, keeping it alive for future generations.

Amaretti

Amaretti, crisp and crunchy, have an intense almond flavour and are gluten-free. They are always on hand at Tuna Nui for Pip to enjoy with friends.

Prep time: *10 minutes*
Cook time: *15 minutes*
Makes: *about 36 biscuits*

1 cup ground almonds
¾ cup desiccated coconut
1 cup caster sugar
¼ cup cocoa, sifted, optional
2 egg whites

Preheat the oven to 150°C (130°C fan bake). Set the rack in the centre of the oven or, if using two baking trays, place a rack either side of the centre to ensure even cooking. Line 1–2 trays with baking paper.

In a large bowl, stir together the almonds, coconut, half the caster sugar and all of the cocoa, if using.

In a second, scrupulously clean bowl, beat the egg whites until they are frothy and beginning to form a foam. Gradually beat in the remaining caster sugar to make a thick, glossy, meringue-like mixture. Stir in the dry ingredients. Place teaspoonfuls on the prepared tray/s, leaving room for the biscuits to spread.

Bake in the preheated oven for 15 minutes or until slightly hard to the touch. Turn the oven off and leave the biscuits inside with the door shut until quite cool.

Stored in an airtight container, these will keep well for 2–3 weeks. If they become soft, place on an oven tray and reheat in the oven at 150°C (130°C fan bake) for 5–8 minutes or until they become crisp through.

Apricot Pistachio Chocolate Slice

A hedonistic and truly decadent slice that is even more delicious if you use a very rich dark chocolate and unsalted butter.

Prep time: *15 minutes*
Chill time: *overnight*
Makes: *40 pieces*

395-gram can sweetened condensed milk
500 grams chocolate (preferably dark), chopped
100 grams butter, diced
1 cup dried apricots, chopped
½ cup shelled pistachios, unsalted and unroasted
¼ cup crystallised ginger, finely chopped

Line the base and sides of a shallow-sided 18cm x 28cm slice tin (or similar), with baking paper.

Put the condensed milk, chocolate and butter in a microwave-proof bowl – preferably glass – and heat in the microwave on high for about 3 minutes or until the mixture is hot. Stir well to combine and if the chocolate or butter has not yet melted, heat in the microwave in small bursts until melted (do not over-heat). Stir in the apricots, pistachios and ginger and mix well. Spread out in the prepared tray, to about 2–2.5cm thick. Refrigerate for 4–5 hours or overnight until the slice becomes firm.

Cut into small pieces with a warm, dry knife. Stored in an airtight container in the refrigerator, this will keep for 3–4 weeks.

When planning to serve, remove from the refrigerator 30 minutes beforehand as the flavours will be better appreciated if not too cold.

COOK'S TIP
- If you like, blanch the pistachios quickly in boiling water, drain and peel. They will be a vibrant green colour. Dry on paper towels before using.

Gluten-free Christmas Cake

At Christmastime, Pip always has one or two well-matured, rich fruit cakes ready to cut to celebrate the season. Pip advises to make this gluten-free recipe well in advance, not just to allow time for the flavours to mellow, but also to reduce the stress that inevitably happens in busy homes as the festive season draws near!

Prep time: *40 minutes*
Cook time: *4–5 hours*
Makes: *20cm cake*

250 grams butter, softened
½ cup white or soft brown sugar
¼ cup liquid honey
6 eggs, beaten
⅓ cup brandy or sherry
1 teaspoon each vanilla and almond essence
1 teaspoon baking soda
½ teaspoon baking powder
grated rind and juice of 1 orange
600 grams ground almonds
500 grams raisins
250 grams currants
250 grams sultanas
125 grams mixed peel
125 grams glacé cherries, chopped
150 grams flaked almonds for decorating

Preheat the oven to 120°C. Set the rack just below the centre of the oven. Grease the base and sides of a 23cm square or round cake tin. Line the base and sides with two layers of brown paper or baking paper. Wrap the outside of the cake tin in several layers of newspaper.

Beat the butter, sugar and honey together until the mixture is very light and creamy. Beat in the egg a little at a time – do not rush or the mixture will split.

Stir together the brandy or sherry, essences, baking soda, baking powder and orange rind and juice.

Stir the ground almonds, raisins, currants, sultanas, mixed peel, glacé cherries and the brandy or sherry mix into the creamed mixture. Transfer the mixture to the prepared cake tin. Scatter the flaked almonds on top.

Bake in the preheated oven for 4–5 hours or until a skewer inserted into the centre comes out clean. If the almonds begin to brown too much, cover with a piece of baking paper. When the cake is done, remove from the oven and cover with a light, clean tea towel. Set aside until completely cold before lifting the cake out of the cake tin, taking care not to disturb the almonds on top.

Store the cake in an airtight container. It will keep well for at least 4–6 weeks.

Spiced Butter Biscuits

Spices lace a simple, delicate butter biscuit recipe to create a sweet morsel that, once sandwiched with a buttery ginger icing, evokes the baking in northern European countries.

Prep time: *15 minutes*
Chill time: *30–60 minutes*
Cook time: *15 minutes*
Makes: *24 joined biscuits*

2 cups flour
1 cup soft brown sugar
1 teaspoon baking powder
2 tablespoons ground cinnamon
2 teaspoons mixed spice
250 grams butter, softened but not melted
1 egg, beaten
Ginger Butter Icing (see recipe on page 265)

Preheat the oven to 180°C (160°C fan bake). Set the rack in the centre of the oven or, if using two baking trays, place a rack either side of the centre to ensure even cooking. Grease 1–2 baking trays or line with baking paper.

Into a food processor, put the flour, sugar, baking powder, cinnamon and mixed spice and pulse to mix. Add the butter and egg, and pulse until the mixture forms a mass. Turn out onto a lightly floured bench and bring together. Wrap in plastic wrap and refrigerate for 30–60 minutes to allow the dough to become firm.

On a lightly floured bench, roll the dough out to 0.3–0.5cm thickness. Cut out into 5cm circles and place on the prepared tray/s.

Bake in the preheated oven for 15 minutes or until the biscuits begin to feel firm to the touch. Transfer to a cake rack to cool. The biscuits will become crisp as they cool.

Once cool, sandwich two biscuits together with ginger butter icing. Stored in an airtight container, these biscuits will keep well for 7–10 days.

Passion for Paua

Life on Arapawa Island for twins Sarah and Jacob Radon (17) and their brother James (14) has echoes of Arthur Ransome's adventure series *Swallows and Amazons*, although the Radon youngsters do at least as much work as play; if hard workers are the key to success, the entire family, with parents Mike and Antonia, surely qualifies. They work as a team in their paua farming enterprise and on the 700-acre farm.

Gunyah, the 1945 homestead, sits high above Whekenui Bay at the entrance to the Tory Channel, with an ever-changing vista across Cook Strait. Dolphins play regularly in the channel and, around Christmas, orca have come right up to the beach in pursuit of stingrays.

Antonia, a nomadic New Zealander, met Mike in California where they were diving for sea urchins (kina). On a brief trip to New Zealand, they fell in love with Whekenui, once the nerve centre of the country's last operational whaling station. With kina returns falling, and feeling that they were ready to settle down, Mike had the instinct that the quality of the waters off the property would be ideal to farm paua. For six years they continued living on their boat and diving to raise the capital for their dream venture, commuting from California to Arapawa.

Their first project was restoring Gunyah, constructed by boat builders for the Perano family, who were whalers. It had been empty for 12 years but Antonia wanted to recreate the original style of the house and stripped all the woodwork back with methylated spirits from dark lacquer to heart rimu. She says it was only the pleasure of seeing the rimu come back to life that kept her going on the thankless task! The result of their labours over five years is a comfortable home with décor that takes its holidaymaking occupiers back some 70 years, albeit with mod cons.

With the arrival of the twins, the Radons refurbished the farmhouse situated on the flats back from the shore, because it was bigger and more convenient for the paua farm buildings. Although still redolent of the 1950s, its kitchen has been modernised, and the front rooms look out over a lovely garden – the 1800s kauri toolshed in the adjacent paddock was the hut for the keeper of the leading lights for navigation. The Radons have also restored and updated the old schoolhouse and the teacher's cottage for holiday accommodation, and they have a dormitory for WWOOFers (Willing Workers on Organic Farms).

Supplies come from Picton, usually on the twice-weekly mail boat, although the family is largely self-sufficient thanks to Antonia's vegetable garden, their own meat and eggs and plentiful fish caught by line or spear fishing, since all of the family are keen divers – a prerequisite for the paua operation.

The paua are housed in sheds, seawater pumping into the tanks through an ingenious bucket system to mimic the movement of ocean currents. The immature paua are 'seeded' into corners in the rocks below the ocean to continue to grow. For Antonia, the 'icing on the cake' is being able to put the baby paua back into the sea, having nurtured them to that stage. She just wishes that people diving for paua would understand the importance of leaving the smaller ones to mature.

Antonia and Mike's most recent project is growing paua pearl, inserting a tiny nucleus disc that irritates the paua into covering it with a hard shell. It takes three years for the pearls to grow. They are a beautiful colour – blue is most prized – and make attractive jewellery. This has led to stricter selection for quality in the grown paua; culls go to restaurants.

Antonia has home-schooled the three children in the purpose-fitted schoolroom, takes tour and school groups around the paua enterprise and looks after the holiday accommodation. Her days start at 5 a.m. in the paua farm and don't finish until late, with school from 7 a.m. until lunchtime. Jacob is doing NCEA Level 2 and Sarah is progressing with ITO agricultural training. She's the farmer, overseeing some 80 beef cattle and 200 easy-care Wiltshire sheep, which are meat animals that don't need to be shorn.

For the past 10 years, Mike has left the farm at the end of summer for Alaska, to chase the sockeye salmon run on their own 32-foot boat, and now Antonia and the children (with school work) join the adventure. It's three frantic weeks of near 24/7 hard labour, sleeping on the boat, but the rewards are worth the effort.

Despite the relative isolation of island life, there's no shortage of contact with other people, no time to be bored, and none of the family shows signs of wanting to change their lifestyle.

Agueda's Bread

Antonia brought this recipe back with her from her travels to Alaska, where each year she and the family go to fish on the famed sockeye salmon run. The bread, which requires only one rise, has a soft crumb and crust, and due to the higher than usual salt quantity, remains moist and toasts up beautifully. It also freezes well.

Prep time: *40 minutes*

Rising time: *20 minutes*

Cook time: *18–20 minutes*

Makes: *1 large loaf or 2 small loaves*

2½ tablespoons active yeast mixture
3 tablespoons sugar
1 cup warm water, plus extra as needed
5 cups flour
1 cup wholemeal flour (or use ½ cup oats and ½ cup chopped nuts)
3 tablespoons salt
4–5 tablespoons oil

In a bowl or large jug, stir together the yeast, sugar and water and set aside for 10–15 minutes until frothy.

Stir the flours and salt in a large bowl. If using oats and nuts rather than wholemeal flour, stir those through now. Make a well in the centre and pour in the frothy liquid and oil. Using a wooden spoon or spurtle, begin to stir together, adding more warm water until you have a sticky dough.

Turn out onto a lightly floured bench and bring together. Shape into a tight round and place the dough on a greased baking tray, cover with a lightly floured, clean tea towel and set aside for 20 minutes to rise. If wished, the dough can be divided into two loaves.

While the dough is rising, preheat the oven to 180°C (160°C fan bake) and set the rack just below the centre of the oven.

Bake in the preheated oven for 30–35 minutes or until the bread sounds hollow when tapped underneath. Transfer to a cake rack to cool.

Serve sliced. This is delicious eaten fresh, accompanied with cheese.

COOK'S TIPS
• For this recipe make sure you use a dried yeast mixture that includes bread improvers, such as Surebake active yeast mixture.
• This recipe has a higher than usual salt content, which may be due to the recipes origins, where there may be a taste for the saltier loaf. The recipe would also work well with half the amount of salt.

Gunyah's Pancakes

The morning routine for the Radons on Arapawa has changed little over the years. Once, the children were woken up early to begin their school lessons in mathematics and English before breakfast; now, with their schooling days coming to an end, the children still wake up early but they go to work before a hearty morning breakfast in which pancakes have a starring role.

Prep time: *10 minutes*
Cook time: *10 minutes*
Makes: *6 pancakes*

> ¾ cup flour
> 2 tablespoons sugar
> ½ teaspoon salt
> ½ teaspoon baking soda
> ½ teaspoon baking powder
> 1 egg
> 1 cup milk
> 50 grams butter, melted

Sift the flour, sugar, salt, baking soda and baking powder into a bowl and make a well in the centre. Beat the egg and milk together and pour into the well. Using a whisk, stir the ingredients together to make a smooth batter. Stir in the butter.

Melt a small knob of butter in a frying-pan over a moderate heat and, when hot, pour in a third of a cup of the batter at a time to cook. When bubbles appear on the surface of the pancake, turn it over and cook the underside for a further minute or so. Transfer to a plate and repeat process with the remaining batter.

Serve the pancakes when freshly cooked, or keep warm in a low oven until all the batter has been cooked. Enjoy with thick Greek-style yoghurt, fruit and maple or golden syrup.

....

COOK'S TIP
- These pancakes freeze well. Stack the cooked pancakes with a sheet of baking paper between each one. Store in the freezer in a sealable plastic bag. Reheat individual pancakes in the microwave.

....

Dutch Apple Cake

In late summer, when Antonia's fruit trees are laden, she will often prepare a fresh fruit cake such as this spiced apple cake. Pears make a great substitute for apples here. To add a typical European baked-goods flavour to the cake, use cassia in place of cinnamon.

Prep time: *20 minutes*
Cook time: *1 hour*
Makes: *24–25cm cake*

    1½ cups flour
    1 teaspoon baking soda
    1 teaspoon ground cinnamon
    ½ teaspoon mixed spice
    ½ teaspoon salt
    1 cup sugar
    1 cup raisins or sultanas
    ½ cup walnuts, chopped
    2 medium apples, peeled, cored and thinly sliced
    150 grams butter, melted
    1 egg, beaten

Preheat the oven to 160°C (140°C fan bake). Set the rack in the centre of the oven. Grease the base and sides of a 24–25cm cake tin and line the base with baking paper.

Into a bowl, sift the flour, baking soda, cinnamon, mixed spice and salt. Stir through the sugar, raisins or sultanas, walnuts, apple slices, butter and egg and stir well to mix thoroughly. Transfer to the prepared cake tin.

Bake in the preheated oven for 1 hour or until a skewer inserted into the centre comes out clean. Cool in the tin for 15 minutes before turning out onto a cake rack to cool.

Dust with icing sugar, cut into thin wedges and serve with cream or custard.

Keep this cake in an airtight container in a cool place, away from sunlight and warmth. Being very moist, it is best enjoyed within 5–7 days.

Tuff Stuff

This recipe must be a favourite, for the scrappy piece of paper on which it is written lives permanently stuck to the fridge door with magnets – always a good indicator of a recipe's place within a family!

Prep time: *20 minutes*
Cook time: *about 25 minutes*
Makes: *16–20 pieces*

2 cups self-raising flour
1 cup desiccated coconut
1 cup soft brown sugar
250 grams butter, diced or grated

Topping
395-gram can sweetened condensed milk
2 tablespoons golden syrup
2 tablespoons butter
¼ cup finely sliced crystallised ginger
¼ cup chopped dark chocolate
¼ cup chopped walnuts

Preheat the oven to 180°C (160°C fan bake). Set the rack in the centre of the oven. Grease the base and sides of a 20cm x 30cm slice tin.

Put the flour, coconut and brown sugar in a bowl and rub in the butter. Press into the base of the prepared slice tin.

Bake in the preheated oven for 15–20 minutes or until lightly browned around the edges.

While the base is cooking, put the condensed milk, golden syrup and butter in a small saucepan and warm, without boiling, until the butter has melted. Pour the condensed milk mixture over the cooked base and scatter the ginger, chocolate and walnuts on top. Return to the oven for a further 6–8 minutes or until the topping has set.

Allow to cool before cutting into pieces to serve. Stored in an airtight container, this slice will keep well for around 14 days.

COOK'S TIP
- Nuts are high in oils, and if kept in a warm, sunny place will become rancid. Store nuts in the fridge or freezer to keep them fresh.

cuits

Stuff

loaf raising
coco
brow
bu

Agg

5

180
ti
2 th
2

Pow

Gng

cups Flow
Oat
nuts
Salt
Oil

granny smith

unbeaten

Put all   a bowl —
Add melted   Add unbeaten,
egg last.

Bake 70 minutes at 300°.

I find with my oven it is

Cranberry Anzac Biscuits

Studded with deep crimson-hued dried cranberries, Antonia's chunky Anzac biscuits recipe is simply delicious.

Prep time: *30 minutes*

Cook time: *15–18 minutes*

Makes: *about 24 biscuits*

1 cup flour
1 cup soft brown sugar
1 cup desiccated or thread coconut
1 cup rolled oats
½ cup slivered, flaked or finely chopped almonds
½ cup dried cranberries
125 grams butter
2 tablespoons golden syrup
½ teaspoon baking soda
2 tablespoons water

Preheat the oven to 180°C (160°C fan bake). Place a rack either side of the centre of the oven to ensure even cooking. Grease two baking trays.

In a large bowl, stir together the flour, sugar, coconut, oats, almonds and cranberries and make a well in the centre.

In a saucepan over a low heat, melt the butter and golden syrup together.

Dissolve the baking soda in the water and stir into the butter mixture. Pour into the dry ingredients and mix well. Roll large tablespoonfuls of the mixture into balls about the size of a small apricot and place on the prepared trays, leaving room for the biscuits to spread. Using the palm of your hand, flatten the biscuits a little.

Bake in the preheated oven for 15–18 minutes, or until the biscuits are golden and have spread and risen a little. Transfer to a cake rack to cool.

Stored in an airtight container, these biscuits will keep for 2–3 weeks.

Lemon and Poppy Seed Muffins

Many of Alison Holst's books compete for space with ingredients on the shelves of Antonia's pantry, and this recipe, developed from one in Alison's *More Marvellous Muffins*, is a favourite with the family.

Prep time: *15 minutes*

Cook time: *12–15 minutes*

Makes: *12 muffins*

2 cups self-raising flour
1 cup sugar
½ cup poppy seeds
2 eggs, light beaten
100 grams butter, melted
grated rind of 2 lemons
1 cup milk

Glaze
juice of 2 lemons
¼ cup caster sugar

Preheat the oven to 200°C (180°C fan bake). Set the rack in the centre of the oven. Grease 12 standard muffin tins or line with paper cases.

Sift the flour into a bowl. Stir in the sugar and poppy seeds and make a well in the centre.

In a jug or separate bowl, beat the eggs, butter and lemon rind together. Pour into the well with the milk, and, using a holed mixing spoon, gently stir together. Do not beat, as this will cause the muffins to peak when they bake. Divide the mixture between the muffin cups.

Bake in the preheated oven for 12–15 minutes.

While the muffins are cooking, make the glaze. Stir the lemon juice and sugar together – the sugar should not dissolve.

When the muffins are cooked, remove from the oven and brush with the sugary glaze. Cool for a few minutes before serving.

Muffins are best enjoyed on the day they are made, though they will keep well for 2–3 days in an airtight container. If stored, reheating in a warm oven before serving will freshen them up.

Tides of Change

In memory of these men
who lost their lives
during the operation of the whaling station at Fishing Bay
between 1924 and 1964

Heteraka "Truck" Herangi
1894 - 1924

John Donald Huntley
1912 - 1943

Gilbert Jones
1906 - 1944

William Herbert Gillice
1889 - 1950

Kei te tio tō huka
I runga i ngā hiwi
Kei te moe koromeke
Te wairua e-i

The sharp bite of the seaspray
carries foam to the tops of hills
but sleeping warm and curled up
is your spirit within me

Churning seas and wild winds often mark the entrance to Tory Channel from Cook Strait, which makes it a difficult place for a keen gardener, but Lisa Heberley cannot imagine living anywhere other than Arapawa Island. Heberleys have lived in the area for seven generations, four of them at Okukari Bay, fishing, whaling and farming.

The place and the people have been recorded by Lisa's mother-in-law, Heather, in five books. *Weather Permitting* chronicled her life as a young wife with four children on an island with no mod cons and a husband often away fishing. The weather hasn't changed for the residents above the bay at the tip of the Marlborough Sounds, even if the mod cons have, and the sea still rules their lives.

Lisa and James met at school in Blenheim. She came to Okukari 26 years ago, when she was 22. She home-schooled their two children, Haydn and Danielle, until they went to boarding school.

'I don't find it hard to be on the island,' Lisa reflects. 'I am never bored, even when James is away.' She's a keen knitter and does 'crafty' sewing and mosaic art and, of course, the garden takes up a fair chunk of time. 'You just have to grow what you can,' says Lisa. Between the cruel north winds that destroy plants and the southerlies that bring burning salt spray, it's a balancing act, and the more tender plants have stronger ones for protection. Adding to the garden's attraction are old fence posts, items from the old whaling station, driftwood and other bits and pieces turned into sculptures, as well as lichen-covered rocks. The vegetable garden and tunnel house provide lots of variety for the pot.

James is a real hunter–gatherer, enjoys recreational fishing for the table and is also a keen pig hunter. 'We eat a lot of wild pig,' says Lisa.

The island is James' and his brother Joe's base for their main occupation of fishing the coast, south to the Clarence River and as far north as Kapiti, for crayfish, groper and shark. The brothers' forebears pursued larger denizens of the deep as whalers; Joe Senior was a gunner on whaling boats in his teens. Numbers declined and the last whale was landed at the factory two bays around from Okukari in 1964.

Joe Sr and fellow old-timers from the industry are still looking for whales, but now they do it for a month from a cosy hut high above the channel entrance, as part of a DOC annual survey to assess numbers as the humpbacks swim north to breed. All are delighted that there's been a marked increase in the animals. It's not only the old whalers who can spot; while the *Country Calendar Homestead Baking* team was with Lisa, she suddenly pointed, 'Look, whales!' Sure enough, much to our excitement, a school of orcas swam into the bay and played around the wharf before heading north.

When James and Joe Junior aren't fishing, they work on the farm, which carries a merino flock – the wool is contracted to Icebreaker. When it comes to shearing, it's all hands on deck, with Lisa, James and Joe's wife Joy on the wool table and Joe Jr on the presser. Heather is the classer, with Joe Sr as the 'gofer'.

Each family has its own house; the original homestead, built in the 1800s, was where Joe and Joy's house now stands. Lisa and James are next door, with Heather and Joe Sr further up the hill. All have views to die for down Tory Channel. On the rare occasion when the whole family is home, it's a busy place – Heather and Joe Sr have 10 grandchildren and six great-grandchildren between the families of their two sons and two daughters.

Heather, Lisa and Joy are all enthusiastic cooks. Heather says she goes by her own mother-in-law's mantra: 'Don't ever change a recipe the first time you use it. Once you have made it, then you can change it.' Lisa learned to cook at home from her mother. 'I love to cook, but I don't use recipes much. I love to see food being eaten and enjoyed.' Her airy kitchen opens onto the dining area and family sitting room, which in turn open onto a deck overlooking the extensive garden, which rings to the sound of tui and bellbirds. It's a relatively modern home, dating from 1988, and holds many mementoes of the family's history: artefacts, shells and suchlike that Lisa has collected.

Okukari Bay is about generations of a family and a long succession since the early days of whaling. It's not an easy life for the men who go fishing or the women who wait at home, but it's a life none of them regrets, nor would they exchange it for an easier berth on the mainland.

Seedy Bread

Lisa's seedy bread, with its crispy outside crust and moist crumb, is absolutely delicious. The flavour and texture come from soaking the seeds overnight, a trick that Lisa says makes the seeds easy to digest as they will be softer when cooked. This recipe will make two generous-sized loaves and the bread freezes well.

Soaking time: *overnight*
Prep time: *30 minutes*
Rising time: *30 minutes*
Cook time: *40–50 minutes*
Makes: *2 loaves*

3 teaspoons salt
about 3 cups seeds (use a mixture of linseed, sesame, pumpkin or
    sunflower seeds, or use rolled oats)
1 tablespoon honey
1 tablespoon molasses (or use golden syrup)
900ml very hot water
4 teaspoons active yeast mixture
½ cup warm water
1 teaspoon sugar
600 grams wholemeal flour
600 grams high-grade flour

In a large bowl, stir together the salt, seeds or oats, honey, molasses or golden syrup and very hot water. Set aside at room temperature overnight.

The next day, grease two large (21cm x 11cm) loaf tins.

Mix the yeast, warm water and sugar together. Set aside until frothy.

Add the frothy mixture to the seed mixture. Stir in the flours and mix with a wooden spoon or spurtle to make a sticky dough. Divide the mixture between the prepared tins. Set aside in a warm place to rise for 30 minutes. You do not want the dough to double in bulk, but it should rise about a quarter to a third in size.

While the mixture is rising, preheat the oven to 200°C (180°C fan bake).

Bake in the preheated oven for 40–50 minutes or until the bread sounds hollow when tapped underneath. Transfer to a cake rack to cool.

This bread is better left for a day before slicing. It will stay moist for several days, and it is also delicious toasted. Store in a bread bin.

COOK'S TIPS
- For this recipe make sure you use a dried yeast mixture that includes bread improvers. Lisa used Surebake active yeast mixture.

Olive Biscuits

Baking never lasts long at the Heberleys'. While they are geographically isolated, they have many visitors. In July, the migration season for whales, the family is joined by teams of whale watchers – locals, DOC staff and volunteers – so Lisa keeps the tins filled with good, simple baking to send up to the whale-watching station. These sweet biscuits do not contain olives, but they are so entrenched in the family's culture that no one can remember the origin of the name. They are enjoyed by the whale watchers and Lisa's family alike.

Prep time: *20 minutes*
Cook time: *15 minutes*
Makes: *about 24 biscuits*

125 grams butter
½ cup sugar
2 teaspoons golden syrup
1 teaspoon baking soda
1 tablespoon milk
½ cup sultanas or raisins
2 cups flour

Preheat the oven to 180°C (160°C fan bake). Set the rack in the centre of the oven or, if using two baking trays, place a rack either side of the centre to ensure even cooking. Grease 1–2 baking trays or line with baking paper.

In a saucepan over a low heat, stir together the butter, sugar and golden syrup until the butter has melted. Remove from the heat.

Dissolve the baking soda in the milk and stir into the butter mixture with the sultanas and flour. Roll teaspoonfuls into balls and place on the prepared tray/s, leaving room for the biscuits to spread.

Bake in the preheated oven for 15 minutes, or until the biscuits are just firm to the touch. Transfer to a cake rack to cool.

When cold, store in an airtight container. These will keep for 2–3 weeks.

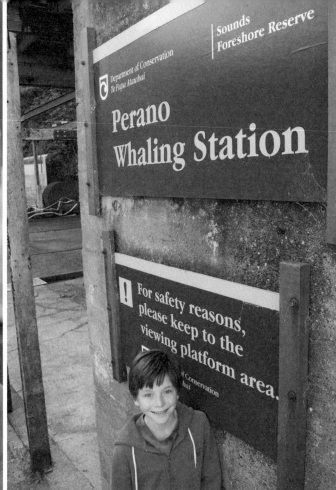

Fly Cemetery

A classic slice – with a hard-to-forget name – that is much-loved by James. The 'flies' are the sultanas or currants used to make the filling and the cemetery is the pastry that sandwiches them together. Home-made fly cemetery far exceeds commercial brands and, when served warm with custard, it doubles as a dessert. Modernise this traditional recipe by using dried cranberries and blueberries in place of the currants and sultanas.

Prep time: *40 minutes*
Cook time: *25–30 minutes*
Makes: *30 pieces*

Pastry
3 cups flour
½ teaspoon salt
250 grams butter, chilled and diced
about ½–⅔ cup water

Filling
1½ cups water
1 cup currants
1 cup sultanas
½ cup sugar
1 teaspoon ground cinnamon
juice of 1 lemon
2 tablespoons cornflour
milk or beaten egg to glaze
2–3 teaspoons caster sugar

To make the pastry, sift the flour and salt into a bowl and rub in the butter. Using a dinner knife, cut in sufficient water to bring the mixture together to form a firm dough. Turn out onto a floured bench and bring together.

Roll out the dough to make a rectangle that is three times longer than it is wide. From the short edge, fold the dough over itself, taking it two-thirds of the way up. Bring the top portion over so that you have three layers of pastry. Give the dough a quarter turn, and repeat this rolling and folding process twice more. Wrap in greaseproof paper or plastic wrap and refrigerate until ready to use.

Preheat the oven to 200°C (180°C fan bake). Set the rack in the centre of the oven. Line the base and sides of a 20cm x 30cm slice tin with baking paper.

To make the filling, put the water, currants, sultanas, sugar, cinnamon and lemon juice in a saucepan and bring to the boil. Lower the heat and simmer for 5 minutes. Mix the cornflour with a little water to make a smooth paste and stir into the hot fruit. Continue stirring over a moderate heat for 1–2 minutes or until thickened. Allow to cool.

To assemble the fly cemetery, divide the pastry in half. On a lightly floured bench, roll one half out large enough to line the base and sides of the prepared tin. Brush the edges with milk or beaten egg and spread the cooled fruit mixture on the pastry.

Roll the remaining piece of pastry out just large enough to cover the top of the tin. Place over the fruit filling and press the pastry edges together firmly, trimming if required. Brush the top with milk or beaten egg and sprinkle with a little caster sugar.

Bake in the preheated oven for 25–30 minutes or until the pastry is golden and well cooked. Cool in the tin before cutting into squares.

Store in an airtight container away from heat and sunlight, and enjoy within 2 weeks.

Mum's Lemon Sultana Cake

This trouble-free basic cake recipe is given new life by Lisa, with a generous flavouring of lemon essence. Another option would be to flavour with lemon oil or use a good tablespoonful of grated lemon rind.

Prep time: *30 minutes*
Cook time: *45–60 minutes*
Makes: *20cm cake*

500 grams sultanas
250 grams butter, diced
2–3 teaspoons lemon essence
1½ cups flour
1 teaspoon baking powder
3 eggs, at room temperature
1 cup sugar
1 quantity Lemon Butter or Simple Vanilla Icing (see recipe on page 265)

Preheat the oven to 180°C (160°C fan bake). Set the rack in the centre of the oven. Grease the base and sides of a 20cm round or ring tin. Line the base with baking paper.

Put the sultanas in a saucepan and just cover with water. Bring to the boil, then lower the heat and simmer for 8 minutes. Strain well and return to the saucepan. Stir in the butter and lemon essence and continue to stir until the butter has melted. Set aside to cool for 10 minutes.

Sift the flour and baking powder together and set aside.

Using electric beaters, beat the eggs and sugar together until thick and creamy. Stir into the fruit mixture alternately with the flour. Transfer to the prepared cake tin.

Bake in the preheated oven for 45–60 minutes or until a skewer inserted into the centre comes out clean. Stand in the cake tin for 10 minutes before turning out onto a cake rack to cool.

When cold, ice with lemon butter icing, slice and serve.

Stored in an airtight container, this cake will keep well for about 2 weeks.

Steamed Jiffy Pudding

Steamed puddings hot from the pudding bowl, their soft porous texture soaking up any cream poured on, are one of life's pleasures. As preferred by the Heberleys, dried fruit and spices stud this easy-to-make recipe.

Prep time: *20 minutes*
Cook time: *1½ hours*
Serves: *6–8*

1 cup flour
1 teaspoon baking powder
1½ cups mixed dried fruit
½ cup sugar
2 tablespoons butter
1 teaspoon mixed spice
1 teaspoon baking soda
1 cup boiling water

Fill a large saucepan or stockpot one-third full with water and place an old saucer in the bottom to act as a trivet. Bring the water to the boil.

Grease a 4–5-cup capacity pudding bowl.

Sift the flour and baking powder together and set aside.

In a bowl, stir together the dried fruit, sugar, butter, spice, baking soda and boiling water, mixing until the butter melts. Stir in the sifted dry ingredients.

Transfer the mixture to the prepared pudding bowl. Cover with two layers of greased baking paper and one layer of foil. Secure by tying with string under the lip of the bowl.

Carefully lower the pudding bowl into the saucepan or stockpot. The water should be boiling, and it must come about two-thirds of the way up the sides of the pudding bowl. If not, add more boiling water from a kettle. The water in the saucepan must not come off the boil. Simmer the pudding for 1½ hours, topping up the water level as required.

Remove the pudding bowl from the water and allow to stand (still covered) for 3–5 minutes before turning out to serve. This is best served hot, accompanied with ice cream and/or whipped cream.

Leftover slices will reheat easily in the microwave – allow 30–60 seconds per serving-sized slice.

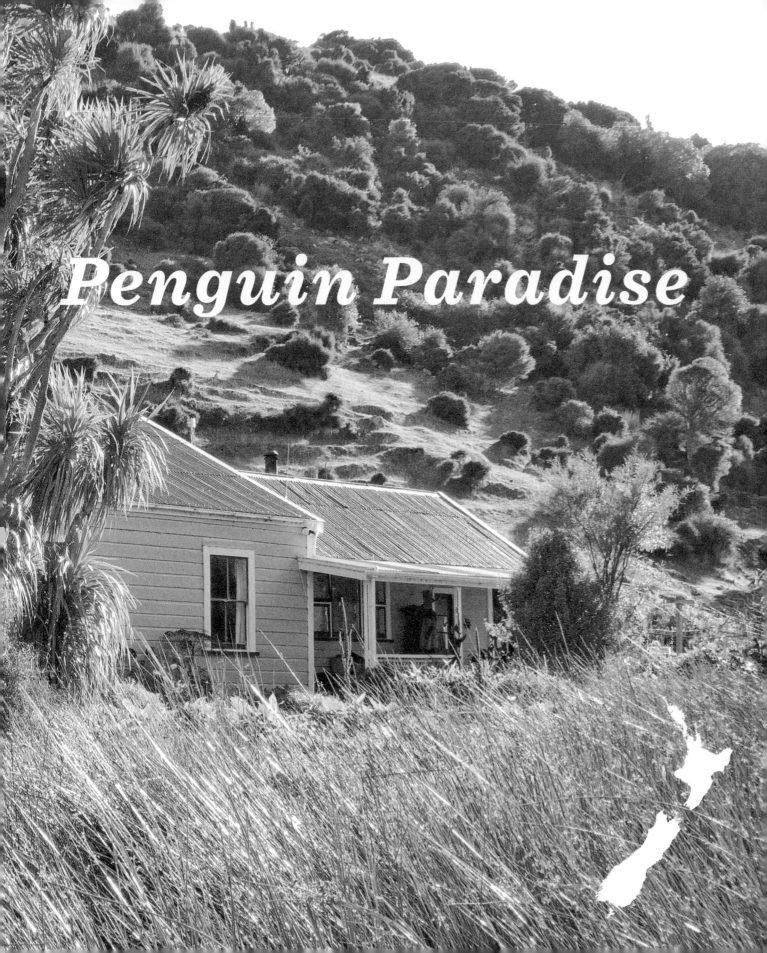

Penguin Paradise

As the crow flies, Flea Bay is not far from Akaroa but, driving to the southeast tip of Banks Peninsula over a narrow shingle road with steep drops, it feels like the end of nowhere. Francis and Shireen Helps have lived on the 500-hectare sheep and beef hill farm for 40 years, initially in partnership with Francis's brother Stephen, but now Stephen farms nearer Akaroa, and the Helps and their son Danny run Flea Bay.

Some people claim to have fairies at the bottom of their garden... Francis and Shireen have penguins all over theirs! Nothing gives them more pleasure than in the breeding season, when some of the 1300 breeding pairs of the endangered little white-flippered penguins that call the area home roll up from the beach to take up residence in natural burrows or in the 300 nesting boxes built around the homestead.

It's a marked reversal from the 1970s, when the population in their bay was in sharp decline. The couple set out to eliminate predators – ferrets, stoats, rats, mice, hedgehogs and feral cats. Now they reap the rewards of their persistence... although getting up at three in the morning to stop two males warring loudly over a female under the bedroom window would somewhat dilute the glow of success!

The penguins have enabled the Helps to set up a tourism venture, bringing mostly overseas visitors to Flea Bay by 4WD vans to see the rich wildlife – penguins, seals, Hector's dolphins, land- and sea-based birds and even the rare local geckos. For those who want to get up close in the surrounding Pohatu Marine Reserve, Shireen has a fleet of kayaks.

In 1989, along with other farmers, Francis and Shireen created the Banks Peninsula Track. Flea Bay has accommodation in a 150-year-old cottage for trampers, who now come in large numbers annually. The HQ is a shop in Akaroa, for which Shireen makes handcrafts for sale – notably scarves and hats from the wool of her small flock of coloured sheep, which roam freely around outside the garden along with wild geese and plump black hens. It's a family affair, with her daughter, Joey, and a niece also involved in the tourist business.

Shireen's a woman of many parts – over five years she built a sod cottage just 'to feel what it must have been like for the first people here to build something out of nothing'. Named Rhodes Cottage in tribute to the original family, it is a delightful retreat up the valley from the shore, and is a replica of the first house built on the property in the 1830s.

On the walls of the homestead are numerous paintings, many executed by Shireen or her mother. Joey told us, 'Everybody on both sides of the family are good artists. Mum's won prizes for her painting. Dad is very good at drawing nudes!'

The homestead is one of two similar houses built for members of the Rhodes family at the end of the 1870s, as far as Francis can determine. They believe it was a mail-order or catalogue house, constructed from North Island timber, with kauri shiplap weatherboards, matai flooring and rimu framing. 'It probably cost less than 100 pounds – and it certainly wasn't designed to last for 120-plus years,' says Francis. The rear part of the house, including the kitchen and utility rooms, was added in 1942. The Helps have since made it look like an older colonial cottage with the main house attached. Inside and out, it is painted in the style of the times – all features are picked out in three earth-based colours, with alternate colours for the verandah iron. The interior décor reflects the period, with stained glass in the doors, an original light fitting in the sitting room and a kauri fireplace, rediscovered behind green paint. Other than that, Francis says, 'We have stopped the house falling down!'

It's easy to tell by the numbers of Tilley lamps and candlesticks that the power supply is a tad unreliable at times; and the wood-burning wetback stove is a blessing. 'It blows really hard here,' says Shireen. 'The last big blow demolished a shed that was anchored with bolts, tearing it out of the concrete.' The wind doesn't help the gardening – just another of the tasks this extraordinary couple tackle – but in spring the garden's a riot of colour, making it all worthwhile.

Joey's Chocolate Wedding Cake

Fashions change – even with wedding cakes, and today's preference usually involves chocolate and lots of it. Joey, with help from her mum Shireen, made this recipe to celebrate her wedding day, and it tasted as good as it looked!

Prep time: *20 minutes*

Cook time: *60–70 minutes*

Serves: *10*

2 vanilla beans
200 grams butter
250 grams dark chocolate (minimum 50% cocoa)
1 cup hot black coffee (plunger-style is best)
2 cups sugar (caster is best)
1½ cups flour
¼ cup cocoa
1½ teaspoons baking powder
2 eggs, beaten

Piped Chocolate Topping
100 grams dark chocolate

Preheat the oven to 150°C (130°C fan bake). Set the rack in the centre of the oven. Grease the base and sides of a 20cm square cake tin and line the base with baking paper.

Split the vanilla beans lengthwise and scrape out the seeds. Place the seeds and beans in a saucepan with the butter, chocolate and coffee and warm over a low heat until the butter has melted. Add the sugar and continue to stir until the sugar has dissolved. Remove from the heat and cool. Remove the vanilla beans.

Into a large bowl, sift the flour, cocoa and baking powder and make a well in the centre. Pour in the cooled chocolate mixture and stir gently to mix. Gently stir in the beaten eggs, being careful not to over-mix. Pour into the prepared tin and level off.

Bake in the preheated oven for 60–70 minutes or until a skewer inserted into the centre of the cake comes out clean. Leave in the cake tin for 15 minutes before turning out onto a cake rack to cool.

To make the chocolate topping, melt the dark chocolate, either in the microwave or in the top of a double saucepan. Transfer to a piping bag fitted with a small nozzle. Pipe the chocolate onto a baking paper-lined tray, making patterns to your liking. Transfer to the refrigerator to chill for 15–20 minutes until hard. The chocolate patterns will lift easily from the baking paper.

Serve the cake dusted with icing sugar and decorated with piped chocolate topping.

Keep in an airtight container and enjoy within 7 days.

Golden Dyer Cookies

Golden Syrup Cookies

Given how many times we struck variations of this classic farmhouse biscuit, we suspect its origins must lie in the pages of a well-loved publication of the day such as the *Edmonds Cookery Book*, the *New Zealand Woman's Weekly* or a Country Women's Association cookbook – or maybe even all three. Wherever it came from, it certainly was the most favoured piece of baking we came across while on tour, and was loved by many generations. Shireen's recipe is laden with mixed dried fruit and spiced with plenty of ginger.

Prep time: *15 minutes*
Cook time: *10–12 minutes*
Makes: *about 24 cookies*

250 grams butter, softened
1 cup and 2 tablespoons sugar
1 generous tablespoon golden syrup
2 eggs, at room temperature, beaten
2 cups mixed dried fruit (or use sultanas)
4 cups flour
2½ teaspoons baking powder
1 teaspoon ground ginger
¼ teaspoon salt

Preheat the oven to 160°C (140°C fan bake). Set the rack in the centre of the oven or, if using two baking trays, place a rack either side of the centre to ensure even cooking. Grease 1–2 baking trays or line with baking paper.

Beat together the butter, sugar and golden syrup until the mixture is very light and creamy. Beat in the eggs, one at a time. Stir in the dried fruit.

Sift together the flour, baking powder, ginger and salt and stir into the creamed mixture – it should remain soft. Roll dessertspoonfuls into balls and place on the prepared tray/s, leaving room for the cookies to spread. Flatten slightly with the palm of your hand.

Bake in the preheated oven for 10–12 minutes, or until the biscuits become browned around the edges. Transfer to a cake rack to cool.

Stored in an airtight container, these cookies will keep well for 2–3 weeks.

COOK'S TIP
- If you don't have a cup measure, weigh the flour. For recipes in this book 1 cup of flour is equal to 125 grams.

Clifford Tea Biscuits

Shireen has no idea how far back in her family this recipe goes as it has been handed down through at least four generations that she can recall, and the recipe, albeit converted from imperial to metric, has always remained the same. As for the name, that one is lost to history too.

Prep time: *15 minutes*

Chill time: *overnight*

Cook time: *12–15 minutes*

Makes: *about 24 sandwiched biscuits*

150 grams butter, softened
¾ cup sugar
2 eggs, beaten
2¼ cups flour
½ teaspoon baking powder
¼ teaspoon baking soda
¼ teaspoon ground ginger
¼ teaspoon ground cinnamon
¼ teaspoon salt
1 quantity Basic Butter or Simple Vanilla Icing (see recipe on page 265)

Beat the butter and sugar together until light and creamy. Add the egg a little at a time, beating well, until all the egg has been incorporated.

Sift together the flour, baking powder, baking soda, ginger, cinnamon and salt and work into the creamed mixture. Turn the dough out onto a lightly floured board and bring together. Divide into two or three portions and roll each portion into a log about 4–5cm in diameter. Wrap each portion in baking paper and refrigerate overnight.

Preheat the oven to 180°C (160°C fan bake). Set the rack in the centre of the oven or, if using two baking trays, place a rack either side of the centre to ensure even cooking. Grease 1–2 baking trays.

Cut the logs into 0.5cm slices and place on the prepared tray/s.

Bake in the preheated oven for 12–15 minutes or until the biscuits turn a pale golden colour. Transfer to a cake rack to cool.

When cold, join with icing of your choice and dust with icing sugar to serve.

Stored in an airtight container, these will last up to 2 weeks.

Call of the Hills

Life in the high country of the South Island is often harsh, dominated by the weather, but there's something very special about it – majestic mountains, unique braided rivers, pristine air that whips your breath away on a cold morning. The people who live in these lonely, dramatic places are also special because they need to be tough enough to cope. The pioneers here must have been brave, strong and resourceful.

Driving the roads and crossing the fords to Erewhon Station, at the headwaters of the Rangitata River, west of Ashburton, it's hard not to think of *Lord of the Rings* – and, indeed, Mt Sunday along the way was transformed into the mythical Edoras, capital of Rohan in *The Two Towers*, and Erewhon provided the jaw-dropping background scenery.

Colin Drummond took up the leasehold in 1998. He'd always wanted a high-country place, having worked on several including Molesworth. He says, 'One of the reasons I bought the place was to get away from people – and here I am doing tourism!' The tourism side of the business is down to his partner, Erin Cassie, who has been on the station for six years.

Erewhon is largely about horses nowadays, in a reversion to the past – big, handsome Clydesdales, the horses that helped break in New Zealand. Colin first fell for Clydesdales as a young man, and now has some 60 horses, including stallions, brood mares, youngsters and the working team. For the centennial of the Clydesdale Horse Society of New Zealand, he famously hitched 20 horses to a wool wagon – spectacular!

There are few machines on this property – most tasks are done by real horsepower, and the Clydesdales never freeze up in winter! The horses are also safer for crossing the rivers that run through the station and, as Erin says, 'If they think it's too dangerous, they let you know.' Gung-ho 4WD drivers sometimes think going through the river is a cinch . . . only to find themselves towed out by Clydesdales!

The 14,000-hectare station carries merino sheep, Hereford cattle and deer. There are 120 acres of river flats for growing winter feed, then the property rises from the home farm in the river valley at 620 metres above sea level to 2150 metres high on rugged peaks, running back to the edge of the Main Divide of the Southern Alps, and it is all mustered on horseback or on foot. Colin is looking at more sustainable farming. 'If we only have 80 years left of nitrogen-based fertilisers, we need to be getting the stock used to tougher grasses.'

'Places like this are not terribly profitable,' he says, 'which is why we have gone for tourism. It's sustainable and the market can only grow.' The horses, landscape and outdoor activities are the visitor attractions and they mainly have overseas travellers, often from cruise ships in the summer. They are taken on a wagon ride drawn by three or six horses and brought back to the woolshed for refreshments. Riding experiences are also on offer, as are overnight wagon rides to one of the musterers' huts. The self-contained homestead has four bedrooms, sleeping up to 18, so is ideal for families or groups.

The horses go to shows and ploughing matches and are a huge attraction. Colin says there's a growing interest in the past, including interest in Anzac Day. 'They want to learn about things their grandparents and great-grandparents did and how they lived.' Older people get quite nostalgic, according to Colin.

The 140-year-old homestead on the property is crumbling, and the cost of restoring it would be prohibitive. Plus it was built in a cold spot – backing into a hill and getting little sunshine, especially in winter, when the sun is not on the house until 10.30 a.m. and disappears at 2.30 p.m. The 100-year-old homestead, now used for visitors, has been added to several times. Colin and Erin's own home was a one-bedroom cookhouse, but has been extended.

Prior to taking up high-country living, Erin was a school-teacher. She learned most of her cooking skills from her grandmothers, Dot and Queenie, whose school lunchboxes were legend. 'I was the most popular girl in school because the others wanted to share my lunch.' Hers was a big family – she is the youngest of seven – so there was lots of baking. However, Erin is quite candid about preferring to be out working with the horses than indoors cooking or doing housework!

EREWHON STATION
HOME OF THE WORKING HORSE

RURAL PROPERTY No
2846

Tangoes

Jam-packed with dates and walnuts, these are great cookies for dunking in a cuppa at any time; and a real favourite come shearing time.

Prep time: *15 minutes*
Cook time: *15 minutes*
Makes: *about 24 cookies*

125 grams butter
½ cup sugar
2 tablespoons golden syrup
2 eggs, beaten
2 cups flour
1 teaspoon baking soda
¾–1 cup chopped dates
¾–1 cup chopped walnuts

Preheat the oven to 180°C (160°C fan bake). Set the rack in the centre of the oven or, if using two baking trays, place a rack either side of the centre to ensure even cooking. Grease 1–2 baking trays.

Beat the butter, sugar and golden syrup together until light and creamy. Beat in the egg a little at a time – do not rush or the mixture will separate. Sift the flour and baking soda together and stir into the creamed mixture with the dates and walnuts.

Place tablespoonfuls of mixture onto the prepared tray/s, leaving room for the cookies to spread.

Bake in the preheated oven for 15 minutes. Transfer to a cake rack to cool.

When cold, store in an airtight container. Tangoes will keep well for 2–3 weeks.

Walnut Fudge Grandma Cassie

½ cup butter
1 tsp B.Powder
1 Tbsp chopped walnuts
1 cup flour
2 Tbsp top milk

Walnut Pride

Erin's high school Home Science cookbook folder, complete with hand-written entries from her and others, is her bible at Erewhon. It is filled with simple ideas that can be whipped up using pantry staples, as is the need on this very remote station.

Prep time: *15 minutes*

Cook time: *15–20 minutes*

Makes: *18–20cm cake*

125 grams butter, softened
⅓ cup sugar
2 tablespoons sweetened condensed milk
1 egg, at room temperature, beaten
1 cup flour
3–4 tablespoons chopped walnuts, plus extra to garnish

Topping
50 grams butter, softened
¼ cup icing sugar
1 tablespoon sweetened condensed milk
dash of vanilla essence

Preheat the oven to 160°C (140°C fan bake). Set the rack in the centre of the oven. Grease the base and sides of an 18–20cm square cake tin and line the base with baking paper.

Beat the butter, sugar and condensed milk together until creamy. Add the egg, a little at a time, until well beaten and the mixture is light. Sift the flour and stir into the creamed mixture with the walnuts. Spread the mixture into the prepared tin.

Bake in the preheated oven for 15–20 minutes or until the cake is firm to the touch.

While the cake is cooking, beat all the topping ingredients together. Spread the topping onto the hot cake and scatter over some extra walnuts. Allow the cake to cool before cutting into pieces.

Stored in an airtight container, this cake will keep well for 7–10 days.

Spiced Marble Cake

As a child, Erin remembers the delight of cutting into her birthday cake each year, eager to discover which colours had been used to make the always-requested marble cake to celebrate her special day. Back then, the colours were much more subdued, with little more than cochineal and cocoa to create the marble effect. Today, the selection is far more avant-garde!

Prep time: *20 minutes*

Cook time: *45–55 minutes*

Makes: *20cm cake*

175 grams butter, softened
¾ cup caster sugar
2 teaspoons golden syrup
3 eggs, at room temperature, beaten
2 cups flour
1 tablespoon cornflour
1 teaspoon baking powder
few drops food colouring of choice
1 teaspoon mixed spice

Preheat the oven to 160°C (140°C fan bake). Set the rack in the centre of the oven. Grease the base and sides of a 20cm round or square cake tin and line the base with baking paper.

Beat the butter, sugar and golden syrup together for about 10 minutes, until very light and creamy. Beat in the egg a little at a time. The mixture should be very thick and creamy.

Sift the flour, cornflour and baking powder together and fold into the creamed mixture. Divide the mixture into three equal portions. Leave one portion plain, colour one portion with the food colouring and flavour the remaining portion with the mixed spice. Spoon the three mixtures into the prepared tin and run a knife through to mix the colours and flavours up a little.

Bake in the preheated oven for 45–55 minutes or until a skewer inserted into the centre comes out clean. Cool in the tin for 10 minutes before transferring to a cake rack to cool completely.

Ice and decorate as wished (see page 265 for icing recipes).

Chocolate and Lemon Steamed Pud

A simple family pudding whose complementary flavours are boosted by a sweet, sharp lemon sauce. If planning a meal for more than four, this recipe doubles easily – just add an extra 30 minutes' cooking time.

Prep time: *15 minutes*
Cook time: *1½ hours*
Serves: *4*

75 grams butter, softened
¼ cup sugar
2 eggs
1 cup self-raising flour
grated rind of 1 lemon
1 tablespoon cocoa, sifted

Lemon Sauce
grated rind and juice of 1 lemon
1 cup water
2 tablespoons sugar
2 teaspoons cornflour

Fill a large saucepan one-third full with water and place an old saucer in the bottom to act as a trivet. Bring the water to the boil.

Grease a 3–4-cup capacity pudding bowl.

Using an electric mixer, beat the butter, sugar, eggs and flour together for 1 minute. Divide the mixture in half, flavouring one half with lemon rind and mixing the cocoa into the other half. Spoon the mixtures alternately into the prepared pudding bowl. Cover with a greased layer of baking paper and a layer of foil. Secure by tying with string under the lip of the bowl.

Lower into the saucepan of boiling water, making sure the water comes two-thirds of the way up the sides of the pudding bowl. Cover and steam for 1 hour. Carefully remove the pudding bowl from the saucepan, uncover and transfer to a serving platter.

To make the lemon sauce, heat the lemon rind and juice, water and sugar together in a saucepan. Mix the cornflour with a little water to make a smooth paste and stir into the saucepan and cook, stirring, until thickened.

Serve the pudding warm with lemon sauce.

On the Right Track

Graeme Duncan is a walking history of the Maniototo Plain in Central Otago; not surprising since his forebears took up land in White Sow Valley, Wedderburn, in 1894. Follow the Pig Route (SH85) from Palmerston, through an area redolent with goldmining and farming history, and you come to the Maniototo Plain. It's flat, but it boasts dramatic scenery that blows people away.

After the gold and wool booms, the little towns of the Plain languished, then the railway, which had opened up Central Otago from 1870–1990, closed, and the future looked bleak. However, the descendants of hardy pioneers and goldminers don't quit easily, and foremost among several initiatives was the 152-kilometre Otago Central Rail Trail, opened in 2000, which follows the railway route from Clyde to Middlemarch. Places that were dying are now bustling, as cyclists, riders and walkers from all over the world discover this stunningly beautiful area. There were doomsayers who said it wouldn't work – Graeme says he had severe doubts – but it has changed the Duncan family's business, as well as those of others, as the potential of tourism to bolster incomes and bring the region back to life was increasingly recognised.

Penvose Farm has always been a family affair, and now the fourth, fifth and sixth generations of the family call it home. Graeme is semi-retired, turning the main responsibility over to son Stuart ('Stu'). Stu and his wife, Lorraine, have three children – all dead keen on the farm. Daughter Ellie (16) is at boarding school in Dunedin and Mitchell (14) will be the fourth generation of the family to attend Otago Boys' High, as will Todd (11) in his turn. Mitchell has been mustering since he was seven and Todd is shaping up well.

The 5500 acres carry a well-known Angus stud, deer and flocks of crossbred and halfbred sheep; the family also has an equity partnership in a dairy farm. The other major enterprise is tourism.

The first homestead was built in 1896 on the adjacent block known as Laurieston. The Maniototo was treeless, so much of the early building was with sundried brick – made on the farm of mud, straw and tussock – on a base of schist. The house and outbuildings are now derelict, to Stu's regret, but he says that preservation should have been undertaken decades ago and the cost now would be astronomical. The original two-storey stables building has been restored, as have a couple of other buildings at the steading, all made from the same materials.

Graeme and his wife Alison live in Penvose (the name is Cornish) homestead, which was built further down the farm in 1926 by Graeme's grandfather. True to its period, the lounge and hallways are lined with imported English oak panelling and the doors have leadlight windows. It has five bedrooms, a large lounge and a big dining/living area, and the front rooms have bay windows looking out over the Maniototo to the Hawkdun range. The ceilings are moulded. Alison had the kitchen remodelled to open it out for a family dining and sitting room. Originally, what is now the kitchen was two pantries and the lot was painted dark brown. Now it's bright and airy. Christmas is fun at Penvose, when all the family, including 12 grandchildren, gathers.

While day-to-day farming goes on as always – including an annual bull sale and fulfilling a wool contract with SmartWool, which makes fine apparel – Lorraine and Alison take care of a burgeoning tourist enterprise headquartered at Wedderburn village, where the rail trail, at its highest and halfway point, crosses Penvose land a paddock back from the road.

There are 14 cosy self-contained cottages, The Lodge – a refurbished 1928 farm homestead for groups and families – camping facilities and the Red Barn Visitors' Centre, where Lorraine and Alison welcome their guests. They have hosted conferences and corporate team-building events. The barn is also the pick-up area for tours of the farm and around the district. Golf is available on the farm's own 'challenging' nine-hole golf course, which was Stu's brainchild: 'It's very casual. You can take your dog and you're allowed to swear!' Across the road from the Penvose complex is the 1885 stone Wedderburn Hotel; once a coach and wagon stop, it now offers a warm country welcome to twenty-first-century travellers.

It's changed days for the Duncans, who admit the tourism business was a real learning curve, but they realised that if they didn't do something, someone else would. Now tourism rivals the wool cheque in the farm's coffers.

Cracker Christmas Cake

This perfectly named fruit cake is unbelievably easy to make. Literally you throw it all together in a bowl and stir. The end result is a dense, moist, fruit-laden, gently spiced, classic fruit cake that tastes as divine as it looks.

1.5 kilograms mixed dried fruit
½ cup brandy, whisky, sherry or fruit juice
300 grams butter, well softened but not melted
1 cup soft brown sugar
1 green apple, peeled, cored and grated
4 eggs, beaten
1 tablespoon golden syrup
1¼ cups flour
½ cup self-raising flour
1 teaspoon ground cinnamon
1 teaspoon mixed spice
½ teaspoon ground cloves

Marinating time: *overnight (fruit)*

Prep time: *30 minutes*

Cook time: *3–3½ hours*

Standing time: *2 weeks*

Makes: *23cm cake*

In a large bowl, put the dried fruit and toss with the brandy, whisky, sherry or juice. Cover and leave overnight.

The next day, preheat the oven to 150°C (130°C fan bake). Set the rack just below the centre of the oven. Place a small container, full of water, on the bottom rack in the oven.

Grease the base and sides of a 23cm round cake tin and line with two layers of baking paper. Wrap three to four layers of newspaper around the outside of the tin, securing with string. This will help prevent the outside edge of the cake overcooking.

Stir the butter, sugar, apple, egg and golden syrup into the fruit mixture. Sift the flours and spices together and stir into the fruit mixture. Pack firmly into the prepared tin.

Bake in the preheated oven for 3–3½ hours or until a skewer inserted into the centre comes out clean. If the cake begins to brown too much during cooking, cover it with a piece of paper or foil. Remove from the oven and allow it to cool completely in the tin before turning out.

Leaving the cake in the baking paper, wrap in a layer or two of additional baking paper or greased paper and then foil. Set aside in an airtight container for at least 2–3 days before cutting. If possible leave for up to 2 weeks – the cake will mature beautifully and it will be easier to cut. If stored in an airtight container, this cake will keep for a good 2 months.

Ginger Gems

Ginger gems are 'Kiwi as' – apparently we invented them. They are cooked in gem irons, typically a cast-iron tray, with 12 semi-cylindrical moulds. Right now these mini ginger-packed, sweet loaves are having a revival and for good reason; they are not just easier than muffins to make, they contain far less fat and taste wonderful. Old gem irons can often be found in second-hand shops and are worth seeking out.

Prep time: *10 minutes*
Cook time: *10 minutes*
Makes: *12 mini loaves*

2½ cups flour
1 cup sugar
2 teaspoons ground ginger
1 teaspoon mixed spice
2 teaspoons baking soda
1 tablespoon water
1 egg, beaten
1 tablespoon golden syrup
75 grams butter, melted
milk to make a smooth batter

Preheat the oven to 220°C (190°C fan bake). Set the rack in the centre of the oven. Place the gem iron in the oven to preheat while preparing the mixture.

In a bowl, sift together the flour, sugar, ginger and mixed spice and make a well in the centre. Dissolve the baking soda in the water and mix with the egg, golden syrup and melted butter. Pour into the well and stir, adding sufficient milk to make a smooth batter that drops easily from the spoon.

Into each of the hot gem irons, drop a tiny dot of butter. Quickly divide the mixture evenly among the hot buttered gem irons.

Bake in the preheated oven for 10 minutes. Tap out of the gem irons immediately and serve warm with butter.

Jayne's Rolled Oat Squares

This charming recipe comes from a treasured family friend of the Duncans. The condensed caramel filling, much loved by Kiwi families, sits atop a buttery base and is crowned with an oat 'n' coconut crumble – delicious.

Prep time: *20 minutes*

Cook time: *30–35 minutes*

Makes: *24–30 pieces*

Base
1 cup flour
1 teaspoon baking powder
1 cup desiccated coconut
½ cup sugar
125 grams butter, softened
1 teaspoon vanilla essence

Caramel Filling
395-gram can sweetened condensed milk
50 grams butter
2 tablespoons golden syrup

Coconut Topping
50 grams butter
1 tablespoon golden syrup
1 cup desiccated coconut
½ cup rolled oats

Preheat the oven to 150°C (130°C fan bake). Set the rack in the centre of the oven. Grease the base and sides of a 20cm x 30cm slice tin (or similar), and line the base with baking paper.

To make the base, sift the flour and baking powder together and stir in the coconut and sugar. Add the softened butter and vanilla and mix well. Press the mixture evenly into the prepared tin.

Bake in the preheated oven for 15 minutes.

While the base is cooking, prepare the caramel filling. In a saucepan, put the condensed milk, butter and golden syrup and stir over a low heat for 2–3 minutes until the mixture begins to turn a caramel colour. Remove from the heat.

To make the coconut topping, melt the butter and golden syrup together. Stir in the coconut and rolled oats.

When the base is cooked, spread the caramel filling on top and scatter over the coconut topping. Return the slice to the oven and bake a further 15–18 minutes or until the top is golden.

Cool in the tin before cutting into pieces. Stored in an airtight container, this square will keep well for 7–10 days.

Alison's Sultana Biscuits

Alison's joyful personality is reflected in the generations of her family, who share a passion for fun, laughter and hard work – and who like nothing more than sneaking into the kitchen to raid the biscuit tin, where this variation on the classic golden syrup biscuit lies hiding!

Prep time: *20 minutes*
Cook time: *10 minutes*
Makes: *about 36 biscuits*

125 grams butter, at room temperature
⅔ cup sugar
1½ tablespoons golden syrup
3 tablespoons milk, warmed
½ teaspoon baking soda
2 cups flour
1 teaspoon baking powder
1 cup sultanas (or use chocolate chips)
½ cup chopped walnuts, optional

Preheat the oven to 160°C (140°C fan bake). Set the rack in the centre of the oven or, if using two baking trays, place a rack either side of the centre to ensure even cooking. Grease 1–2 baking trays.

Beat the butter and sugar together until creamy. Stir together the golden syrup, warm milk and baking soda and beat into the creamed mixture. Sift the flour and baking powder and work into the creamed mixture with the sultanas or chocolate chips and walnuts, if using.

Roll generous teaspoonfuls of the mixture into balls and place on the prepared tray/s, leaving room for the biscuits to spread. Flatten biscuits with the floured tines of a fork.

Bake in the preheated oven for 10 minutes or until just starting to brown. Transfer to a cake rack to cool.

Stored in an airtight container, these biscuits will keep well for 2–3 weeks.

High-country
Heritage

It's fair to say that until Shrek, the hermit merino wether, made his presence known, Bendigo was not a household name, but the place is steeped in pioneer and goldmining history – it was the richest quartz-reef strike, and it was once a township. Shrek certainly changed life at Bendigo Station and put it on the world map, but the Perriam family was already pivotal in the community and in the wider field of promoting merino wool as a luxury fashion material. The story of the station and the family has been told by John Perriam in *Dust to Gold*, written in the aftermath of the Shrek phenomenon.

John's daughter Christina grew up on the historic station, and, although she now lives in Wanaka, which is more convenient as headquarters for her business, the iconic property still draws her home and she feels a deep connection to it. Indeed, she and her fiancé Callum Grant are planning to get married on the lawn of the lovely garden in front of the homestead, surrounded by a clipped horseshoe-shaped hedge planted years ago by her late mother, Heather, for just that purpose.

The homestead started life as a manager's cottage in the 1930s. In 1967, the then owners added a second storey, kitchen, living room, office and chiller rooms, and created the English gardens and surroundings. In the 1980s, John and Heather created a formal dining room for entertaining, added verandahs, French doors, the kauri staircase and panelling, and extended the kitchen to include a big pantry. There are paintings on the walls, antiques dotted around – John loves collecting old things – photos of champion sheep, family photos, books everywhere and Heather's collection of Copenhagen plates. The result is a large, comfortable and elegant homestead.

Closer to the steading is the original stone homestead, built in 1910, with wooden ceilings and carved beams. The Perriams restored it in 1986, and since then it has hosted many visitors. It is packed with mementoes of the families, people and animals associated with the Bendigo area – and looks as if it has seen some rip-roaring parties around the bar, which is the counter from the old village store, complete with yard measure. 'We would love to turn the house into accommodation,' says Christina.

Christina is quite candid that she's no baker, but says her mother was 'always in the kitchen, and I have lots of memories of making pikelets and scones for the shearers. Mum made a steam pudding that we used to beg her for.' For the *Country Calendar Homestead Baking* team's visit, Christina has her mother's treasured 'red book' containing her recipes, many of which came from friends. In the spacious kitchen/family dining room, which is the heart of the homestead, Christina, a willing and capable Callum, and Allyson make the recipe selection and prepare the goodies, closely attended by Christina's constant companion, West Highland terrier, Mimi.

Over 25 years ago, Heather established a shop in the tiny nearby village of Tarras, selling fine merino wool garments. Christina, who has a diploma and a degree in design specialising in fashion, started designing for the store under the Suprino Bambino (now Little Perriam) and Christina Perriam (now Perriam) labels. The family developed the village further with a delicatessen, gift shop and tearooms and, of course, a Shrek exhibition, turning it from a blip on the map to a trendy destination. Heather's life – as Kate Coughlan, editor of *NZ Life & Leisure* magazine, put it – 'stood for everything that is great about family, friendship and community'.

Looking beyond Tarras, although her flagship store will remain there in the meantime, Christina says, 'I wanted to follow my own life and I wanted to do fashion.' Passionate about her high-country heritage and about the merino fibre she uses, she relaunched her label as simply Perriam last year at a function in the garden at Bendigo – the next step towards her ambition to take her designs and fabrics to a much wider world. The business is irrevocably tied to the rugged high-country environment in which its progenitor grew up and from which Christina takes her inspiration, making it unique.

Olive Oil and Cheese Scones

Callum, who wields a deft hand in the kitchen, believes scones can easily be given a culinary makeover with a touch of Italy. He adds extra virgin olive oil, and blankets the scones in shards of Parmesan and a sprinkling of sea salt before baking – *delizioso*!

Prep time: *15 minutes*

Cook time: *12–15 minutes*

Makes: *12 scones*

2 cups flour
2 teaspoons baking powder
½ teaspoon salt
1 cup milk
¼ cup buttermilk or plain unsweetened yoghurt
¼ cup olive oil (use the best you have)
1 cup grated cheese (try Parmesan or pecorino)

Preheat the oven to 210°C (190°C fan bake). Set the rack above the centre of the oven. Grease a baking tray or line with baking paper.

Sift the flour, baking powder and salt into a bowl and make a well in the centre. Mix together the milk, buttermilk or yoghurt and olive oil and pour into the well. Mix to make a soft, spoonable dough. Spoon 12 portions onto the prepared tray and scatter the cheese evenly on top.

Bake in the preheated oven for 12–15 minutes or until golden and well-risen. Transfer to a clean, cloth-lined basket or cake rack and serve warm.

Scones are best enjoyed soon after cooking, though day-old scones are delicious halved, toasted and buttered.

Bendigo Shortbread

In Heather's recipe book you'll find the original hand-written recipe for this shortbread, well-marked with smears of butter, sugar and flour from many years of being cooked with love. It's hard to pass up an excellent shortbread and Heather's recipe, now prepared by Christina, is a great-tasting traditional version.

Prep time: *15 minutes*
Cook time: *25–30 minutes*
Makes: *36–40 biscuits*

300 grams butter, softened
1 cup icing sugar
2 cups flour, sifted
1 cup cornflour, sifted

Preheat the oven to 150°C (130°C fan bake). Set the rack in the centre of the oven or, if using two baking trays, place a rack either side of the centre to ensure even cooking. Grease 1–2 baking trays or line with baking paper.

Into a large bowl, put the butter and icing sugar and mix well. Gradually work in the sifted flour and cornflour. Turn the dough out and bring together. Divide into two or three portions and form each portion into a log the shape and size of a bar of soap. (At this time, the shortbread logs can be wrapped in baking paper and refrigerated overnight, if desired.)

Cut the shortbread logs into 0.5cm slices and place on the prepared tray/s. Prick the top of each slice three times, using a fork.

Bake in the preheated oven for 25–30 minutes or until beginning to brown a little on the edges. Transfer to a cake rack to cool.

When cold, store in an airtight container. Shortbread will taste better if left to mature for a week before enjoying.

COOK'S TIP
- **Many of our cooks' recipes used terminology that today seems unfamiliar or odd, such as 'the shape of a bar of soap'. Indeed it was, once, a perfectly appropriate guide. For cooks needing a more rigid descriptor, shape the shortbread into blocks about 5cm x 7cm.**

Connie's Coconut Biscuits

Light as a feather and crisp as a wafer, these coconut biscuits are simply charming.

Prep time: *15 minutes*
Cook time: *15–18 minutes*
Makes: *around 24 biscuits*

125 grams butter
¾ cup sugar
1 egg
1 teaspoon vanilla essence or extract
1 cup flour
1 teaspoon baking powder
1 cup desiccated coconut

Preheat the oven to 180°C (160°C fan bake). Set the rack in the centre of the oven or, if using two baking trays, place a rack either side of the centre to ensure even cooking. Grease 1–2 baking trays or line with baking paper.

Beat the butter and sugar together until light and fluffy. Add the egg and vanilla and beat well. Sift the flour and baking powder together and stir into the creamed mixture with the coconut. Drop teaspoonfuls of mixture onto the prepared tray/s, leaving room for the biscuits to spread.

Bake in the preheated oven for 15–18 minutes or until the biscuits are beginning to brown around the edges. Transfer to a cake rack to cool.

When cold, transfer to an airtight container. These biscuits will stay crisp for around 7–10 days.

Caramel Royal Steamed Pudding

As steamed puddings go, this is one of a kind. Taking the condensed milk caramel recipe much-loved by Kiwi cooks, topping it with a delicate batter and steaming it to perfection creates an amazing version of the classic golden syrup pud. Christina remembers having this as a child and, once sampled, it's a pudding that is hard not to wish for again and again!

Prep time: *20 minutes*
Cook time: *1–1½ hours*
Serves: *6*

Caramel Base
½ x 395-gram can sweetened condensed milk
1 tablespoon butter
1 tablespoon golden syrup
2 tablespoons soft brown sugar
½ teaspoon vanilla essence or extract

Pudding
1 cup flour
1½ teaspoons baking powder
½ cup milk
1 tablespoon unsweetened coffee essence
½ teaspoon vanilla essence or extract
1 egg
¼ cup sugar
1 tablespoon melted butter

Fill a large saucepan or stock pot one-third full with water and place an old saucer in the bottom to act as a trivet. Bring the water to the boil.

Grease a 5–6-cup capacity pudding bowl.

To make the caramel base, warm the condensed milk, butter, golden syrup, brown sugar and vanilla in a saucepan over a low heat, stirring constantly. Once the butter has melted, pour the mixture into the prepared pudding bowl.

To make the pudding, sift the flour and baking powder together. Stir together the milk, coffee essence and vanilla. In a large bowl, whisk the egg and sugar together until light and fluffy. Fold in the sifted flour alternately with the milk mixture and the melted butter. Carefully spoon the pudding on top of the caramel base in the prepared pudding bowl. Cover with two layers of greased baking paper and a layer of foil. Secure by tying with string under the lip of the bowl.

Carefully lower the pudding bowl into the boiling water and steam for 1–1½ hours. Keep an eye on the water level, which should come about two-thirds of the way up the pudding basin, adding more boiling water from a kettle if required.

Carefully lift the bowl from the saucepan, uncover and invert onto a serving plate. Cream or ice cream is mandatory with this pudding!

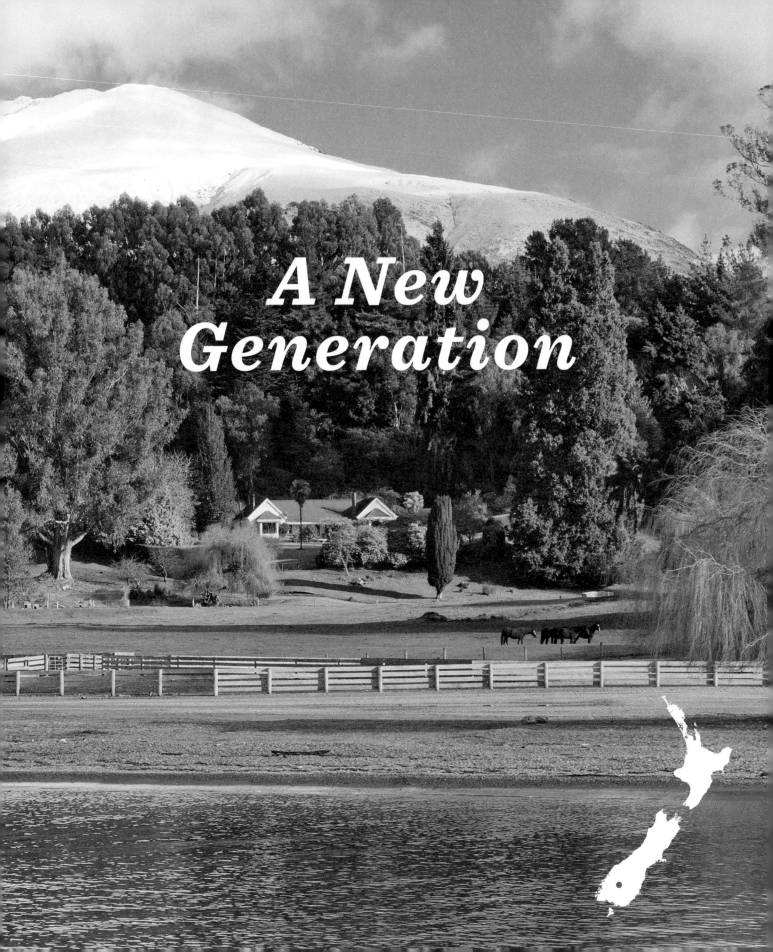

A New Generation

The road into Mt Nicholas Station is not for the faint-hearted – better to arrive stress-free across Lake Wakatipu from Queenstown, taking in the majestic surroundings.

When owners Robert and Linda Butson, who had farmed the 40,000 hectares since 1976, decided it was time to pull back a bit, they looked to their son and daughter. Dave, who had worked with his father on the station for 10 years, decided he wanted to become a full-time commercial helicopter pilot, so it was Kate with her husband, Jack Cocks, who picked up the baton.

Kate and Jack's children Jessica (5) and Tom (3) are the fourth generation to live in the main homestead, built in 1909. The original homestead, dating from the 1850s, was inland by 12 kilometres. 'It's the coldest place on the station,' says Kate. All that remains of the house is the restored stone cookhouse, which features in the tourism and events venture run in conjunction with the farm. It has even been used for a wedding night surprise for a bride. There's no record of her reaction when her groom brought her to the remote spot, but he presumably didn't tell her about the ghost of the cook murdered by her husband who is said to show up from time to time!

The present Mt Nicholas homestead is at the front of the property above the farm buildings on the lakefront. Built from materials salvaged from the dismantling of the original house and an adjoining property, it is a handsome single-storey building with double gables and a tiled roof. Bay windows look over the garden and horse paddock to the lake and mountains. There are still occasional reminders of its origins; during the renovation of a bathroom, when the old panelling was exposed, they found that it was papered with newspapers dating back to the 1860s.

Surrounding the homestead are extensive mature flower and vegetable gardens and an orchard planted at the beginning of last century. Roses, rhododendrons, azaleas and camellias provide wonderful colour, and there are large palms on the front lawn, and red beech and native trees that attract many birds.

The prolific vegetable garden, together with a separate 'paddock garden' for root crops, berry houses, orchard, hens, farm stock and occasional deer, supply food for the 14 people who live on the station. In addition to Kate's family, there is Phil (the head shepherd) and his partner Tish (the station cook), Angus and Brad (shepherds), Bruce Collins and Adrienne McNatty (who manage the tourism), Robert and Linda, and Dave (Kate's brother) and his partner Regina.

It's a heavy responsibility for a young couple but Kate and Jack – who both have agriculture degrees – love farming. The property carries 28,000 merino sheep and 2300 Hereford cattle. The wool goes to clothing manufacturer Icebreaker (Mt Nicholas was their first supplier). The lambs go to Silere Alpine Origin Merino.

Such is the rugged terrain – it rises from 300 metres at the lake to over 2000 metres, encompassing river valleys and flats, tussock country and mountain ranges – that stock work is done on horseback or on foot. Extra staff come in for the 10-day autumn muster – seven men, seven horses and 30 dogs bring in 9000 wethers from the mountain tops before the snow comes. It's classic high-country farming: weather dependent, so good planning is critical, but modern technology also comes into play. As well as spraying ragwort and broom, they are experimenting on control by biological means – bugs and beetles – and it is proving highly successful.

How does Kate cope with the isolation? She reckons the isolation is other people's perception. With visitors, hunters and tourists, there are always people around. 'When you live in a place like this, a lot of people visit.' Apart from fresh food, other supplies come quarterly from Invercargill.

'There are so many fabulous places on the property; it's a wonderful place to live and work,' says Kate. 'Most of what living here entails is organisation – you just have to think in advance, and be efficient when you do go into town. It's all the small things; we are not close to tradesmen, so we have to do most things ourselves.'

Kate loves old china, and pride of place goes to a set of Royal Doulton Rondelay, given by her grandfather to his wife, who added to it before Kate inherited it. She loves cooking and particularly making preserves, chutneys and jams from the garden's bounty. Her well-stocked pantry and storage room have to be seen to be believed! Her baking tins came from Jack's grandmother – 'so much better than the new ones,' says Kate. She home-schools Jess, and Tom's turn will come. How this young woman crams so much into her days is a testament to good organisation and to loving the life the family has chosen.

Coconut Raspberry Square

Linda's personal bake-tin favourite is Louise Slice, which at Mt Nicholas is simply called coconut raspberry square.

Prep time: *20 minutes*
Cook time: *30 minutes*
Makes: *20 pieces*

100 grams butter, softened
½ cup caster sugar
2 egg yolks
⅔ cup flour
¼ cup self-raising flour
1 tablespoon custard powder
¼ cup raspberry jam (or another red fruit jam)

Coconut Topping
2 egg whites
¼ cup caster sugar
1½ cups desiccated coconut

Preheat the oven to 180°C (160°C fan bake). Set the rack in the centre of the oven. Grease the base and sides of a 20cm x 30cm slice tin (or similar), and line the base with baking paper.

Beat the butter and sugar together until well creamed. Beat in the egg yolks. Sift the flours and custard powder together and stir into the creamed mixture. Spread into the base of the prepared slice tin.

Bake in the preheated oven for 15 minutes. Spread the jam over the warm base.

In a clean bowl, beat the eggs whites until thick. Gradually beat in the sugar and, when the mixture is stiff and glossy, stir in the coconut. Spread on top of the jam. Return the slice to the oven for a further 12–15 minutes or until the coconut topping is golden. Cool in the tin before cutting into squares.

Stored in an airtight container, this slice will keep well for 7–10 days.

Davy's Cream Puffs

As a young boy of 12, Dave surprised his family during one school holiday when he whipped up a batch of good old choux puffs – perhaps inspired by a school cooking class. They have forever after remained his favourite and look set to become favourites with his niece and nephew, too.

Prep time: *15 minutes*
Cook time: *40 minutes*
Makes: *about 30 small puffs*

1 cup flour
pinch salt
100 grams butter, diced
1 cup water
3 eggs, beaten

Preheat the oven to 200°C (180°C fan bake). Set the rack in the centre of the oven. Grease a baking tray and sprinkle with a little water.

Sift the flour and salt together and set aside.

Put the butter and water into a saucepan and place over moderate heat so that the butter melts before the water comes to the boil. Once the butter has melted, bring to a full rolling boil. Add all of the flour and, using a wooden spoon, beat quickly to mix everything together to form a ball. Cook for 1 minute, beating constantly. Tip the dough out onto a bench, and leave to cool for a few minutes.

Return the dough to the saucepan and beat in the eggs, a little at a time, until the mixture is thick and glossy; elbow grease is needed here! Alternatively, place the dough in an electric mixer fitted with a K beater and gradually beat in the egg. Place dessertspoonfuls of mixture onto the greased tray, allowing a little room for the puffs to rise.

Bake in the preheated oven for 30 minutes. Do not open the door during this time as the puffs will collapse. When cooked, the puffs should be golden and firm to the touch, almost crunchy. Turn off the oven. Use a small, sharp knife to make a small cut in each puff and return them to the turned-off oven to cool completely.

Store in an airtight container. Serve filled with whipped cream and decorate with melted chocolate or Chocolate Butter Icing (see recipe on page 265).

Fruit Sponge Pudding

Come late spring, throughout summer and then into autumn, when the day's farm work is done, Kate, her family and any workers are kept busy in the orchard, picking fruit from the trees as it comes into season. Soft berry fruits that flourish before Christmas are soon followed by currants – of which Kate has red, black and white – and then it's a non-stop roll to gather in the apricots, plums and peaches. When at last the air turns cool, it is time for apples and pears to be picked, bottled or stewed and frozen. Mt Nicholas Station is pretty much self-sufficient when it comes to fruit, so when a family pud is baked it usually includes fruit – and this sponge is a favourite.

Prep time: *15 minutes*
Cook time: *40 minutes*
Serves: *4–5*

> 2 cups stewed fruit such as apples, pears, peaches or rhubarb
> 125 grams butter, softened
> ½ cup sugar
> ½ teaspoon vanilla essence
> 2 eggs, beaten
> 1 cup self-raising flour
> 2 tablespoons milk

Preheat the oven to 190°C (170°C fan bake). Set the rack in the centre of the oven.

Place the fruit in a 4-cup capacity ovenproof dish and put into the preheated oven to heat through while preparing the sponge.

Beat the butter, sugar and vanilla together until light and creamy. Beat in the egg a little at a time. Fold in the flour alternately with the milk. Remove the dish from the oven and quickly spread the sponge on top of the hot fruit. Return it to the oven and bake for 40 minutes or until the sponge is golden and cooked. Check the centre of the sponge – it should be springy to the touch and feel just firm.

Serve warm with cream or custard.

Madeleines

Madeleines are a personal favourite of Kate who, by her own admission, really prefers to bake only simple recipes with the finest basic ingredients.

Prep time: *15 minutes*

Cook time: *20 minutes*

Makes: *12 madeleines*

2 eggs, at room temperature
½ cup caster sugar
½ cup flour

100 grams butter, melted and
  cooled
grated rind and juice of 1 lemon

Preheat the oven to 200°C (180°C fan bake). Set the rack in the centre of the oven. Grease 12 madeleine moulds.

Using an electric beater, beat the eggs and sugar together until light in colour and fluffy and thick in texture. Sift the flour and fold in alternately with the cooled melted butter and the lemon rind and juice. Divide the mixture evenly among the greased tins.

Bake in the preheated oven for 20 minutes or until golden and firm to the touch. Transfer to a cake rack to cool.

Serve warm, dusted with icing sugar and, if wished, a little grated lemon rind. These are perfect with coffee. Madeleines are best enjoyed on the day they are made, but they will keep in an airtight container for 3–4 days. Freshen them up by placing in a 120°C oven for a few minutes to warm through before serving.

Ginger and Pear Petits Gâteaux

Kate likes to partner ginger and pears and often she will add a touch of cocoa to give a warmer colour that doesn't affect the delicate flavour combination.

Prep time: *20 minutes*

Cook time: *12–15 minutes*

Makes: *12*

125 grams butter, softened
½ cup sugar
1 teaspoon vanilla essence
2 eggs, at room temperature,
  lightly beaten
1 cup self-raising flour

1 tablespoon cocoa, optional
1–2 teaspoons ground ginger
½ teaspoon mixed spice
¼ cup milk
1 pear, canned or stewed

Preheat the oven to 200°C (180°C fan bake). Set the rack in the centre of the oven. Line 12 standard muffin tins with paper cases.

Beat the butter, sugar and vanilla until light and creamy. Add the eggs, one at a time, beating well after each addition. Sift the flour, cocoa, if using, and spices together and fold into the creamed mixture alternately with the milk. Half-fill each of the cases with mixture. Cut the pear into 12 small pieces and place one piece into each mould. Divide the remaining batter evenly among the moulds.

Bake in the preheated oven for 12–15 minutes. Transfer to a cake rack to cool. Serve dusted with icing sugar or drizzled with Chocolate Butter Icing (see recipe on page 265).

Madeleines

Ginger and Pear Petits Gâteaux

Basic Recipes

BASIC BUTTER ICING

100 grams butter, at room temperature
1½ cups icing sugar, sifted
few drops vanilla essence
about 1–2 tablespoons milk

Beat the butter until pale and fluffy. Beat the icing sugar and vanilla into the creamed butter and add sufficient milk to make a soft-textured icing. For an even softer icing, add extra milk.

Variations

Chocolate: Stir 2 tablespoons of cocoa into 2 tablespoons of hot milk until smooth. Allow to cool. Add to the basic recipe. Add extra milk to reach prefered consistency if wished.

Ginger: Add 1–2 tablespoons of finely chopped crystallised ginger, or use 1 teaspoon of ground ginger.

Lemon: Add the grated rind of 1 lemon, and use lemon juice in place of the milk.

SIMPLE VANILLA ICING

1½ cups icing sugar, sifted
25 grams butter, melted
few drops vanilla essence or extract
2–3 tablespoons warm water or milk

Stir together the icing sugar, butter, vanilla and enough water or milk to make a thick but smooth icing that will spread easily.

Variation

Chocolate: Stir 1–2 tablespoons of cocoa into 1–2 tablespoons of warm water or milk. When smooth, stir in the sifted icing sugar, butter, vanilla and enough additional water or milk to make a smooth icing.

CARAMEL SAUCE

½ cup brown sugar
¼ cup golden syrup
¼ cup water
1 tablespoon butter

Stir all of the ingredients together in a saucepan over a moderate heat until the sugar dissolves. Simmer gently for 5 minutes, stirring regularly. For a creamier taste, add ¼ cup of cream when cool.

BASIC CREAM CHEESE ICING

100 grams traditional cream cheese, at room temperature
100 grams butter, at room temperature
1½ cups icing sugar, sifted
few drops vanilla essence, or grated rind of ½ lemon
1–3 tablespoons milk, optional

Beat the cream cheese and butter together until very light and fluffy. Beat in the icing sugar and the vanilla or the lemon rind. If wished, add the milk, a little at a time, to achieve a softer icing.

Variation

Lemon: Add the grated rind of 2 lemons.

Contact Details

TWO IN THE BUSH
Mataia Homestead
www.mataia.co.nz

CHAOS SPRINGS
Chaos Springs Farm
www.chaossprings.co.nz

A DREAM RUN
Glenburn Station
www.glenburnstation.co.nz

HERE TO STAY
Waiorongomai Station
www.waiorongomai.co.nz

RUGGED COAST
Kawakawa Station
www.kawakawastationwalk.co.nz

OUT OF NOWHERE
Blue Duck Station
www.blueduckstation.co.nz

CHANGING THE GUARD
Turihaua Station
www.turihaua.co.nz

UPHOLDING TRADITION
Tuna Nui Station / Tuna Nui Gamebirds
www.nzgamebirds.co.nz

PASSION FOR PAUA
Arapawa Homestead / Arapawa Seafarms
www.arapawahomestead.co.nz

PENGUIN PARADISE
Pohatu Penguins
www.pohatu.co.nz

CALL OF THE HILLS
Erewhon Station
www.erewhonstation.co.nz

ON THE RIGHT TRACK
Wedderburn Cottages
www.wedderburncottages.co.nz

HIGH-COUNTRY HERITAGE
Bendigo Station / Perriam
www.perriam.co.nz

A NEW GENERATION
Mt Nicholas Station
www.mtnicholas.co.nz

Index

Penguin
Random House
New Zealand

First published by Penguin Random House New Zealand, 2016

1 3 5 7 9 10 8 6 4 2

Recipes © Allyson Gofton and individual contributors, 2016

Text © Joan Gilchrist, 2016

Food photography © Alan Gillard, scenery photography © Alan Gillard,
Allyson Gofton and Joan Gilchrist, 2016

Photographs on front cover and this page © Tam West

Cover design by Kate Barraclough © Penguin Random House New Zealand

Text design by Kate Barraclough and Sarah Healey © Penguin Random House New Zealand

Typeset in Sentinel and Ziggurat by Kate Barraclough

Colour separation by Image Centre Group

Printed and bound in China by Leo Paper Products Ltd

A catalogue record for this book is available from the National Library of New Zealand.

ISBN 978-0-14-357348-7

penguinrandomhouse.co.nz